Mastering Devops with Continuous Security:

Advanced Strategies and Best Practices

Copyright Page :

Printed in India

First Printing, 2023

Printer Name:
Imaginary Printer
233, Man Saro Ver Garden,
Nth Floor, New Delhi 110015

ISBN: 978-93-5980-754-6

Publisher Name:
Self-Published

Dedications:

I dedicate this to my fiancée Pragati Gupta. To my brother who motivated me to write the book Vishwajeet Vishnu. To my mentor and colleague, Saurav Agarwal, Vinay Janardhanachari and Animesh Goyal.

To my dearest friend Vishal Singh who has always pushed me to do something extraordinary. Last but not the least, to my grandparents and parents, who always support me and whose blessings have always provided me strength and kept me motivated.

Thank you all for being there for me throughout this journey.

Acknowledgments

Ideally, I would take this opportunity to say thank you to everyone who helped make this book possible. To those who provided moral support, intellectual insights, and technical feedback and facilitated the editing, publishing, and design, I offer my sincere appreciation.

Nobody has had more of an impact on the development of this project than my family. Thank you to my parents and grandparents, whose love and guidance are with me in all of my pursuits. They are the ultimate role model.

I want to thank my loving and supportive fiancee Pragati Gupta, as well as my brother and mentor, who inspired me to write a book, Vishwajeet Vishnu and my dearest friend Vishal Singh who provided unending inspiration.

Last but not least, I ask forgiveness of all those whom I have not named while they have been with me over the years.

About the Book

Explore the dynamic intersection of DevOps and security in our book, 'Mastering DevOps with Continuous Security: Advanced Strategies and Best Practices.' This comprehensive guide takes you on a journey through the evolving landscape of DevOps, equipping you with the expertise needed to excel in today's fast-paced IT environments.

From fostering a security-first culture to mastering advanced strategies like containerization, microservices, and compliance automation, this book equips you with the knowledge and practical insights needed to excel in modern DevOps environments. Discover how to seamlessly integrate security practices, mitigate vulnerabilities, and stay ahead of emerging trends.

Discover the power of Infrastructure as Code (IaC), container orchestration with Kubernetes, continuous integration and deployment, and the intricacies of microservices and cloud-native architectures. We also delve into monitoring, secrets management, continuous security testing, and governance, ensuring you're well-prepared to tackle real-world challenges.

Stay ahead of the curve with insights into emerging technologies, such as AI, blockchain, and edge computing, and explore practical projects for hands-on experience. Whether you're a seasoned DevOps practitioner or just embarking on your journey, this book offers a comprehensive foundation for mastering DevOps with a security-first mindset.

About the author

Meet Sachin Agarwal

Sachin Agarwal is an Author & IT Professional with extensive experience in DevOps, Cloud, Observability, Monitoring and Automations whose accomplishments include:

Education:

- Degree in Information Technology, B.Tech (Hons.) from AKTU (formerly known as UPTU).

Work History:

- 8+ years of experience in DevOps and Cloud.
- Provides Professional Training as Freelancer for DevOps and Cloud.

Publications:

- A Guide To Start DevOps At Any Age : 11

Awards, Titles, Recognition and Designations:

- AWS Solutions Architect Associate Certified (CSA - Associate)
- Certified Kubernetes Administrator (CKA)

Personal Info:

- Currently working as Senior DevOps Engineer in Securonix.
- Worked with Corporates such as Deloitte, IBM, Reuters and Virtusa.
- Write Blogs and posts on Linkedin on different technical topics.
- Cloud & DevOps Enthusiasts
- Worked with multiple clients from different domains and accomplished great honours within the organization.

To be successful in any field or to achieve anything in life, all you need is instruction and encouragement from someone who has "been there and done that!".

Moreover, as you can see from above, DevOps and

Cloud Enthusiasts Sachin Agarwal are uniquely qualified to help you understand everything you need to know about DevOps!

Who should read this book ?

This book is designed for a wide range of people. If you're already working in DevOps and want to get better at it, this book is for you. If you're a security expert but want to understand how DevOps fits in and how to keep things secure, you'll find this book useful too.

DevOps professionals looking to deepen their skills and stay current in a rapidly evolving field will find this book invaluable. It's equally well-suited for security experts seeking to understand the intricacies of DevOps integration and how to secure modern IT environments effectively.

If you're a software developer or engineer and want to integrate security into your daily practices, you will discover a wealth of knowledge on secure coding, vulnerability management, and continuous security testing.

Even if you're a manager or leader in an IT organization, DevOps and security initiatives within your organizations will find this book an essential resource for devising strategies, fostering collaboration, and ensuring compliance.

Moreover, students and educators in computer science and IT-related fields can use this book as a comprehensive learning resource, thanks to its clear explanations and practical examples.

In essence, anyone with an interest in mastering DevOps with a strong emphasis on security, regardless of their level of expertise, will find this book to be an indispensable guide in navigating the complex and ever-evolving landscape of modern IT practices.

How to use this book ?

- **Start with the Basics:** If you're new to DevOps and security, begin with the early chapters. They lay the foundation and introduce fundamental concepts.
- **Choose Your Path:** You don't have to read this book cover to cover. Pick the chapters that align with your interests and needs. For example, if you're keen on containers, go directly to that chapter.
- **Hands-On Learning:** Throughout the book, you'll find practical examples and exercises. Try them out on your own computer or system. Learning by doing is one of the most effective ways to grasp the material.
- **Take Your Time:** Don't rush. Understand each concept before moving forward. If something

isn't clear, re-read the section or seek additional resources online.

- **Use it as a Reference:** Once you've read through the book, keep it on your shelf as a reference. You can return to specific chapters when you encounter real-world challenges in your work.

- **Share and Discuss:** Consider discussing what you've learned with peers or colleagues. Sharing insights and experiences can deepen your understanding and lead to new ideas.
- **Stay Curious:** Technology evolves, so keep your curiosity alive. Stay informed about emerging trends and technologies in DevOps and security, as mentioned in the book's final chapters.
- In essence, this book is your guide to mastering DevOps and security. Use it as a flexible resource to enhance your knowledge and skills at your own pace.

Preface

In today's rapidly evolving tech landscape, the collaboration between Development (Dev) and Operations (Ops) teams, commonly known as DevOps, has transformed the way organizations build, deploy, and manage software. This book is your comprehensive guide to mastering the art of DevOps, with a particular focus on integrating continuous security practices.

My journey into the world of DevOps began over 8 years ago, driven by a passion for streamlining processes, improving software delivery, and enhancing security. Throughout my career, I've had the privilege of working with a wide array of tools, technologies, and talented individuals across diverse industries. This book draws upon that extensive experience to provide you with a roadmap to becoming a DevOps expert.

While "Mastering DevOps with Continuous Security" assumes you have a foundational understanding of DevOps concepts, it goes beyond the basics, delving into advanced strategies, best practices, and the crucial role of security in the DevOps ecosystem.

In these pages, you'll explore topics such as Infrastructure as Code, containerization, microservices, and cloud-native architectures. You'll learn about secure coding practices, vulnerability management, and compliance automation. Moreover, we'll guide you through the integration of security throughout the development lifecycle and show you how to align security and DevOps teams effectively.

Whether you're a seasoned DevOps practitioner looking to expand your expertise or just starting your journey, this book offers valuable insights, practical examples, and real-world scenarios that will empower you to navigate the complex and ever-evolving landscape of DevOps and security.

Our aim is simple: to equip you with the knowledge and skills needed to excel in modern IT environments where DevOps and security are at the forefront. By the end of this journey, you'll be well-prepared to embrace the challenges and opportunities that await in your DevOps career.

Thank you for embarking on this learning journey with us.

Warm regards,
Sachin Agarwal

Table of Contents:

- Building Reusable Infrastructure Components
- Managing Infrastructure as Code in Different Environments
- Implementing Security Controls in Cloud Environments
- Levearing Security-as-Code Principles

6. **Containerization and Orchestration**
    - Introduction to Containers and Docker
    - Container Orchestration with Kubernetes
    - Deploying and Scaling Applications with Containers
    - Best Practices for Container Security and Monitoring

7. **Continuous Integration and Deployment**
    - The Importance of Continuous Integration (CI)

- Application Performance Monitoring and Log Management
- Continuous Monitoring for Security Events

10. Secrets Management and Access Control

- Best Practices for Managing Secrets
- Secure Storage and Encryption of Secrets
- Implementing Role-Based Access Control (RBAC)
- Securing Credentials in CI/CD Pipelines

11. Continuous Security Testing

- Integrating Security Testing into the CI/CD Pipeline
- Dynamic Application Security Testing (DAST)
- Security Scanning for Containerized Environments
- Fuzz Testing and Security Test Automation

12. Security Governance in DevOps

- Establishing Security Governance Frameworks

- Security Policies and Standards for DevOps
- Security Awareness and Training Programs
- Security Metrics and Key Performance Indicators (KPIs)

13. Compliance Automation

- Automating Compliance Checks and Audits
- Implementing Continuous Compliance Monitoring
- Mapping Security Controls to Regulatory Requirements
- Security Compliance Reporting in DevOps

14. **Future DevOps Trends and Emerging**

- DevOps and Artificial Intelligence (AI)
- Blockchain and DevOps Integration
- The Role of DevOps in Edge Computing
- The Impact of DevOps on IoT Security

Database DevOps

Real-World Examples

Top 10 Projects for Practice

Top 10 DevOps Certifications

(Source: www.google.com)

Exam	Certification	Exam Duration and Format	Evaluation
CKA	Certified Kubernetes Administrator	120 Minutes 17 Hands-on practical questions	Indicates the ability to do basic installation as well as configuring and managing production-grade Kubernetes clusters
CKAD	Certified Kubernetes Application Developer	120 Minutes 19 Hands-on practical questions	Indicates the ability to define resources and leverage core Kubernetes primitives for creating, migrating, configuring scalable apps
CKS	Certified Kubernetes Security Specialist	120 Minutes 15-20 Hands-on practical questions	Demonstrates the ability to secure container-based applications and Kubernetes platforms throughout build, deployment, and runtime
TA 003	HashiCorp Certified Terraform Associate	60 Minutes 70 multiple choice / select questions	Demonstrates foundational knowledge of Terraform, including distinctions between Terraform Cloud, Enterprise, and Community
KCNA	Kubernetes and Cloud-Native Associate	90 Minutes 60 multiple choice / select questions	Showcases fundamental Kubernetes and cloud-native expertise, covering kubectl, architecture, components handling, and security
LFCS	Linux Foundation Certified System Administrator	120 Minutes 20-25 performance based tasks	Operates Linux systems, deploys applications, understands key concepts and Linux networking in cloud-native setups.
DCA	Docker Certified Associate	90 Minutes 13 multiple choice & 42 DOMC questions	Certifies Docker containerization expertise across fundamentals, orchestration, networking, security, storage, troubleshooting, and Docker Compose
VA 002	HashiCorp Certified: Vault Associate	60 Minutes 70 multiple choice / select questions	Validates expertise in basic concepts, skills, and use cases related to HashiCorp Vault
EX280	Red Hat Certified Specialist in OpenShift Administration	180 Minutes 15-17 Hands-on practical questions	Demonstrates proficiency in creating, configuring, and managing a cloud app platform with Red Hat OpenShift Container Platform.
EX294	Red Hat Certified Engineer (RHCE) exam (Ansible)	120 Minutes 50-60 multiple choice / select questions	Validates expertise in managing multiple systems with Red Hat Ansible Engine and executing common system administration tasks

CHAPTER 1

INTRODUCTION

The Evolution of DevOps and Security Integration

In the rapidly evolving world of IT and software development, adaptation is not merely a choice; it's a necessity. This chapter marks the beginning of our journey into "Mastering DevOps with Continuous Security," and it starts with a crucial historical perspective-the evolution of DevOps and its intrinsic relationship with security.

DevOps: A Paradigm Shift

Not too long ago, the worlds of software development and IT operations were often viewed as separate entities, each with its own distinct goals, timelines, and methodologies. This separation created bottlenecks, delays, and inefficiencies in the software delivery process. It was clear that a new approach was needed to bridge this gap and streamline the development-to-deployment lifecycle.

Enter DevOps, a transformative philosophy that redefined how teams collaborate, communicate, and automate their workflows. DevOps broke down silos, encouraging developers and operations personnel to work hand in hand. This shift in mindset led to faster development cycles, improved software quality, and enhanced agility in responding to changing business requirements.

The Birth of DevSecOps

As DevOps gained prominence, it became evident that security could no longer be an afterthought in the software delivery pipeline. Cyber threats were becoming increasingly sophisticated, and organizations needed to protect their systems and data throughout the development process. Thus, the concept of DevSecOps was born.

DevSecOps extends the collaborative principles of DevOps to include security teams. It emphasizes integrating security practices into every phase of the software development lifecycle, from design and coding to testing and deployment. This approach ensures that security is not a hindrance but an integral part of the process.

The Continuous Security Imperative

In today's landscape, where data breaches and

cyberattacks are ever-present threats, continuous security has become paramount. Traditional security models, where security assessments occurred periodically, are no longer sufficient. Continuous security involves real-time monitoring, threat detection, and immediate response to security incidents.

This book takes you on a journey through this evolving landscape, where DevOps and security converge to create a dynamic, responsive, and secure software development ecosystem. Our aim is to equip you with the knowledge and tools to navigate this landscape effectively.

As we delve deeper into the following chapters, we'll explore the principles, strategies, and best practices that underpin the modern DevOps and security integration. Together, we'll prepare you to be a master in this ever-evolving field.

Let's embark on this enlightening journey into "Mastering DevOps with Continuous Security."

Evolution of DevOps to DevSecOps

The way we make software has changed a lot. There

used to be DevOps, and now there's something called DevSecOps. This change is a big deal because it shows that companies realize how important it is to have security in every step when making software.

Some really big security problems happened in the past, like when people's personal information got stolen from Equifax, SolarWinds, and Capital One. These events show how bad things can get if we don't do security well.

Now, with DevSecOps, we try to make sure security is a part of everything we do when building software. This way, we can lower the chances of bad things happening, follow the rules better, and make software that is safer and stronger.

This evolution has been driven by several factors, such as:

- **Increased security threats:** with the growing sophistication of cyberattacks, security has become an increasingly important concern for businesses.

- **Greater regulatory demands**: many companies are subject to increasingly strict regulations regarding data protection and privacy.

- **Greater adoption of the cloud**: with the growing adoption of the cloud, security has become a critical aspect in data protection and risk management.

Implementing DevSecOps, it is necessary for all involved teams, including security teams, to adopt practices and tools that enable the integration of security into the **development and operations process**.

Below are the few examples of **High - Profile Security Breaches**:

1. **Equifax Data Breach (2017):** It is one of the largest and most significant data breaches in history. The credit reporting agency Equifax suffered a massive breach that exposed the personal data of nearly 148 million consumers. The breach occurred due to a known vulnerability in a web application framework that was left unpatched. This incident highlighted the need for stronger security practices, including the integration of security into the software development process.

   Reference: □ 2017 Cybersecurity Incident &

Important Consumer Information

2. **SolarWinds Cyber Attack (2020):** The SolarWinds cyber attack was a sophisticated supply chain attack that compromised the software updates of SolarWinds' Orion IT management platform. The attackers were able to infiltrate the networks of numerous high-profile organizations, including U.S. government agencies and Fortune 500 companies. This breach underscored the need for enhanced security measures throughout the development and deployment of software, including thc importance of DevSecOps practices.

   Reference: SolarWinds Update on Security Vulnerability

3. **Capital One Data Breach (2019):** In this breach, a hacker exploited a misconfigured web application firewall to gain access to the personal data of over 100 million Capital One customers. The incident highlighted the importance of securing infrastructure and implementing security best practices throughout the software development lifecycle.

   Reference: Information on the Capital One cyber

incident

Overview of DevOps and Security Principles

In our journey towards mastering DevOps with continuous security, it's crucial to lay a strong foundation by understanding the key principles that govern both DevOps and security practices. These principles form the bedrock upon which successful integration and collaboration are built.

DevOps Principles

- **Collaboration:** At the heart of DevOps lies the principle of collaboration. DevOps breaks down the traditional silos between development and operations teams, fostering communication, empathy, and shared responsibilities. This collaboration accelerates the delivery of software, reduces errors, and enhances overall efficiency.
- **Automation:** Automation is the driving force

behind DevOps. By automating repetitive tasks, such as code deployment and infrastructure provisioning, teams can eliminate manual errors, reduce lead times, and ensure consistency in their processes. This principle also extends to automating security checks and tests to catch vulnerabilities early in the development pipeline.

- **Continuous Integration (CI):** CI is a fundamental DevOps practice where code changes are frequently integrated into a shared repository. Automated tests are run on these changes to detect issues early. CI ensures that code remains stable and ready for deployment throughout the development cycle.
- **Continuous Delivery (CD):** CD builds upon CI by automating the delivery process. It ensures that code can be reliably and rapidly deployed to production. CD pipelines, when designed correctly, include automated testing and security checks to maintain the integrity and safety of deployments.
- **Monitoring and Feedback:** DevOps emphasizes continuous monitoring of applications and infrastructure in production. This real-time feedback loop allows teams to detect issues,

gather performance data, and make informed decisions for improvements. Security monitoring is an integral part of this principle to detect and respond to security threats promptly.

Security Principles in DevOps

- Shift Left: In traditional development, security often came at the end of the process as a final check. In DevOps, security "shifts left," meaning it is integrated into the development process from the very beginning. Security considerations are part of the design and coding phases, ensuring that vulnerabilities are addressed as early as possible.
- **Immutable Infrastructure:** Immutable infrastructure is a security concept that treats infrastructure as code. It means that once an infrastructure component is created, it remains unchanged. If a vulnerability is discovered, instead of patching the component, a new, secure version is created and deployed, reducing the risk of configuration drift and unauthorized changes.
- **Least Privilege Access:** Following the principle of least privilege, individuals and processes should only have the minimum access necessary to perform

their tasks. This reduces the attack surface and limits the potential damage of security breaches.

- **Continuous Security Testing:** Security testing is integrated into the CI/CD pipeline, allowing for automated security scans and vulnerability assessments with every code change. This ensures that security issues are identified and addressed early in the development process.
- **Security as Code:** Similar to Infrastructure as Code (IaC), security policies and configurations are defined as code. This ensures that security controls are consistent, versioned, and can be audited and tracked, just like application code.

Understanding these core DevOps and security principles is essential as we move forward in this book. These principles are the guiding lights that will help you navigate the complex terrain of modern DevOps practices with a continuous focus on security. With these foundations in place, we're ready to delve deeper into advanced DevOps strategies and security integration in the upcoming chapters.

CHAPTER 2

Building a Secure DevOps Culture

In our journey to master DevOps with continuous security, one of the most critical stops along the way is the establishment of a secure DevOps culture. Culture is the bedrock upon which all successful DevOps transformations are built, and integrating security seamlessly into this culture is paramount.

Understanding the DevSecOps Philosophy

DevSecOps is a new work philosophy. DevSecOps is not merely a buzzword; it's a mindset, a philosophy that underpins the integration of security into every aspect of DevOps. It signifies a shift from traditional security approaches, where security was an afterthought or a gatekeeper, to a proactive and continuous security stance.

All organizations, whether large or small, are under constant pressure to increase innovation and accelerate delivery of new products. In order to achieve this, many choose to adopt DevOps to achieve increased flexibility and efficiency.

DevOps has greatly transformed the way organizations work and software development projects are executed. It combines the basic principles of development with a faster and shorter lifecycle approach. DevOps also ensures that functions and fixes are implemented frequently and quickly.

However, if maximum value is to be achieved in relation to the responsiveness and agility of DevOps, security must play an indispensable and integrated role throughout the software development cycle. And this is where DevSecOps comes in.

The importance of safety

The security testing of a software was traditionally

done at the end of the development process, almost at the last minute, and with the intention of launching a product on the market as soon as possible and at the time that was considered most appropriate in order to have an advantage over the competition, leaving aside security.

This worked when software updates and releases were once or twice a year. But as companies adopted Agile and DevOps methodologies, and began migrating to the cloud, those development cycles were reduced to weeks or even days, giving way to an exponential increase in cyber attacks and security breaches that cost companies millions in damages. But in addition to the economic and reputational damage, today there are also the sanctions imposed by governments under laws such as the GDPR.

Given that both the possibility of a cyber attack and the potential damage are greater than ever, there is no better time than now for organizations to start developing additional security capabilities.

The logical extension of the DevOps cultural change to address this need is DevSecOps

What is DevSecOps?

DevSecOps, an acronym for Development, Security and Operations, incorporates security as the main concern and throughout the entire life cycle of software delivery rather than treating it as a separate and potentially optional concern.

Due to the growing need for security in business and the increased use of the DevSecOps methodology, the market size is estimated to increase from $1.47 billion in 2018 to $5.9 billion in 2023, and this figure is expected to reach $13.63 billion by 2026.

Growth of the DevSecOps market
(in billion dollars)

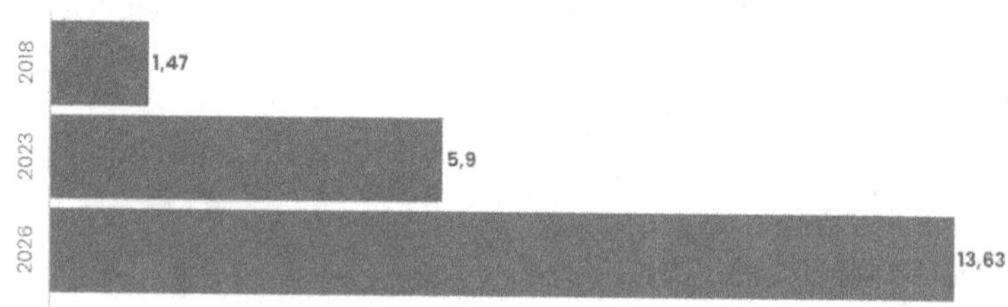

The main objective of DevSecOps is to incorporate security awareness into the whole process of delivering value from software ideation to implementation, delivery and monitoring. It addresses security issues as they arise, when they are still easier, faster and less costly to solve.

In addition, DevSecOps makes application and infrastructure security a shared responsibility of the development, security and IT operations teams, rather than the sole responsibility of a security silo. This enables the delivery of more secure software by automating the delivery without slowing down the software development cycle.

As with DevOps and the Agile methodology, this method is interpreted and implemented in the most efficient way possible, minimising bureaucracy and maximising the delivery value to customers.

In this chapter, we explore the core principles of the DevSecOps philosophy:

Proactive Security: DevSecOps emphasizes the proactive identification and mitigation of security risks throughout the entire software development lifecycle. Security is no longer a checkpoint at the end of a project; it's an ongoing concern.

Shared Responsibility: Every member of the DevOps team, from developers and operations staff to security experts, shares responsibility for security. This collaborative approach ensures that security is everyone's concern, not just a specialized team's.

Automation: Automation is a key enabler of DevSecOps. By automating security checks, vulnerability scanning, and compliance testing, teams can ensure that security is consistently applied and that vulnerabilities are detected early.

Continuous Feedback: The DevSecOps culture thrives on continuous feedback loops. Teams regularly assess their security measures, learn from incidents, and adapt to evolving threats. This feedback-driven approach enhances security resilience.

Fostering a Security-First Mindset in DevOps Teams

To build a secure DevOps culture, it's essential to

cultivate a security-first mindset within your teams. This mindset encompasses the following principles:

Education and Awareness: Ensure that all team members are educated about security best practices and are aware of the potential risks. Regular training and awareness programs are valuable in this regard.

Ownership and Accountability: Encourage team members to take ownership of security concerns in their respective domains. Accountability ensures that security is not someone else's problem but a shared responsibility.

Risk Assessment: Teams should perform risk assessments for their projects. This involves identifying potential security risks, evaluating their impact, and devising strategies to mitigate or manage them.

Secure Coding Practices: Developers play a crucial role in secure DevOps. They must be well-versed in secure coding practices, understanding how to write code that is resilient to common vulnerabilities.

Incident Response Planning: Develop and document incident response plans to ensure swift and effective action in the event of a security incident. Preparedness is key to minimizing the impact of security breaches.

Let's talk about certain scenarios which will make you think that why a security-first mindset is required in any team. Let's look at a few of the case studies which will prove this.

There was a data breach at Bigbasket in October 2021, which sacrificed the information of over 20 million people. Then there was a breach at Juspay, a payment gateway, in which over 35 million people's primary information such as names and addresses, as well as financial details such as card numbers and banking credentials were revealed. In a security breach at Dominos, the data of over one million people was put at risk. Another major breach occurred very recently at Air India, where over 4.5 million people were affected. According to research by IBM, it has been found that the average cost of a data breach is over 5 million US dollars. But what is interesting is that it is about 30 times cheaper to fix the defects during the development stage of software, compared to once it goes out into production. Though this is still a considerable amount of money, at least it saves companies from incurring a bigger loss.

So the people behind the development of DevOps are now fostering a new paradigm or a philosophy, which they term as 'Dev + Sec + Ops' (philosophy of integrated security practices within the DevOps process). This basically integrates security practices with the existing DevOps process and philosophy to make sure that security is the most important aspect in every stage of software development, and not an afterthought.

Some of the tools that are already being put to use in the DevOps toolchain can be used to manage DevSecOps too. No new tools are needed for DevSecOps. Tools such as **Jira, Git, Gradle, and Selenium** are a few that can be used for planning, coding, building and testing software. They are used in DevOps but are compliant with DevSecOps as well — it is just a matter of how they are implemented. Tools such as **Puppet, Chef, and Sensu** can be used for deployment, operation and monitoring.

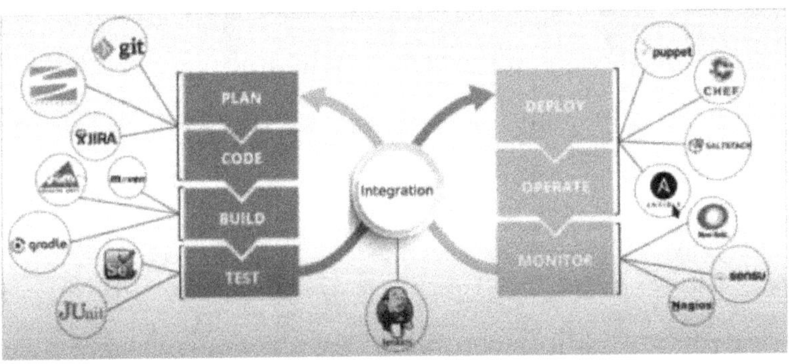

Collaboration between Development, Operations, and Security

One of the central tenets of DevOps is collaboration, and this extends to security. In this chapter, we'll delve into strategies for fostering collaboration between development, operations, and security teams. When these teams work together seamlessly, they can achieve the goal of integrating security into the DevOps pipeline effectively.

As much as the automation of the entire workflow is important, there is an extent to which it can be done using tools. Managing a single server manually is not a big deal, but to manage tens of thousands of servers together every day can be super challenging. A code can be put in place in the form of an application, which can very easily manage these servers on its own. It can be instructed to do so according to the required security protocol. Let us look at some of the benefits of using security as code.

Collaboration: A code is an unambiguous common language that can be understood by literally everyone, even if a person doesn't have any prior understanding of it. Anyone can learn to code and it will perform the same way wherever it is implemented. This makes it significantly easier to work with people from all walks of life.

Scalability: It is highly scalable. Irrespective of the number of servers or nodes being managed, a piece of code is going to perform the same way wherever it has been deployed. This leaves almost no room for error and minimises the risk of malfunctions.

Visibility: Since the code is always visible, it can be edited anytime it is necessary to do so. Whenever there is a bug that might cause any kind of hindrance, it can be rectified very easily without any significant damage. It can be altered at will at any given point of time.

It's a no-brainer that security shall always be the utmost priority for anything that you do on the Web, and anything that comprises system hardware and software. Weak security can lead to irreversible losses. Hence, it becomes imperative for developers to implement foolproof security using evolving philosophies like DevSecOps.

Security Automation and DevOps Workflows

Automation is a linchpin of DevSecOps. We'll also explore how automation can be harnessed to embed security checks, tests, and validation directly into DevOps workflows. This automation ensures that security is consistently applied without slowing down the development process.

According to F5 Labs research, enterprise organizations manage an average of 983 applications, which often span across multiple clouds and data centers. Modern applications are generally designed with distributed architectures and built using agile development practices down to the component level. This framework for continuous integration and continuous delivery (CI/CD) enables DevOps to manage the software lifecycle with both speed and efficiency. With time to market as a primary KPI (key performance indicator), DevOps has adopted modern workflows and automation. Security, however, is often left out of the CI/CD security workflow.

The absence of application security controls in the DevOps workflow means that they are not tested alongside the application code. As a result, application-security defects may not be discovered until operational testing is performed near the end of the development cycle, where addressing flaws is much more costly. The impacts may include significant delays in time to market, higher remediation costs, or inadequate security controls.

Introducing security testing earlier in the CI/CD process is the most efficient solution for addressing the gap between the application and security teams. The challenge is to do it with scale and efficiency, which requires both cultural and technology shifts that emphasize operational security testing as part of the application development phases.

There are few concepts which will help us to

understand how can we implement security workflows into DevOps.

Shift security left

Shifting security left is a key principle of DevOps, which involves incorporating security checks and controls early in the software development lifecycle to identify and fix vulnerabilities before they become more costly and risky to address. To achieve this, you can use tools and techniques such as static application security testing (SAST), dynamic application security testing (DAST), interactive application security testing (IAST), and software composition analysis (SCA). SAST analyzes source code for potential flaws and bugs, DAST simulates attacks on the running application to detect vulnerabilities at runtime, IAST combines SAST and DAST to provide real-time feedback and coverage, while SCA scans dependencies and libraries for known vulnerabilities and license issues.

Automate security tasks

Integrating security into your DevOps workflow can be done by automating security tasks, which can help reduce human errors, save time, and enforce consistency. Automation can be used for code scanning and review, triggered by code commits, pull requests, or merges. Security testing can be integrated into the CI/CD pipeline and run on every build or deployment. Security monitoring and alerting can track the performance and behavior of the application, alerting you of any anomalies or incidents. Lastly, security patching and updating can apply the latest security fixes and updates to the application and its components.

Foster a security culture

The third way to integrate security into your DevOps workflow is to foster a security culture among your team members and stakeholders. This involves educating and training them on security best practices, standards, and tools, as well as involving security experts and champions in the planning, design, and review stages of the project. Additionally, it is important to encourage collaboration and communication between development, operations, and security teams, while also rewarding and recognizing security achievements and improvements. By following these three ways, you can create more secure and reliable web applications. Security is not a one-time event or a separate phase; it is a continuous and integrated process that requires teamwork and commitment.

By now, you should have a solid understanding of how to nurture a secure DevOps culture and why it's the foundation for successful integration of security practices. Building this culture sets the stage for the advanced strategies and best practices we'll explore in the subsequent chapters of this book.

CHAPTER 3

Secure Coding Practices and Static Analysis

When you hire builders to construct a new home, you expect them to take every precaution to ensure once you move in, you won't find split beams, foundational errors, or holes in the walls. In the same way, software developers are expected to uphold secure coding practices to ensure they aren't leaving any vulnerabilities open for hackers to exploit.

One of the biggest problems in computer software today is that most of the softwares or systems have not been built with security in mind. Most of the software security comes from the reactive approach. In some cases our perimeter security technologies like Firewall, IPS and IDS can help reduce the obvious security issues like scripting attacks, injection attacks on servers but they do nothing to address the real security challenges. If we need to solve the computer security problem, we need to do more to build secure software.

Software Security is a practice of building software to be secure and work properly in case of any security attack from attackers. This chapter is all about software security's most important practices.

Engineers are always thrilled to build software from scratch, they are always in so much hurry to make it available to customers without considering software security, which is the most important aspect. We believe that it is the responsibility of the people who create software to make sure that their creations are secure. Software security cannot be left to the system administrator or the end user.

We sometimes meet programmers who question whether software security is a worthy goal. They believe, if no one hacked their software yesterday, why would someone hack it in the future? Security always requires some extra attention, thought, and design effort. Most of the time exploitation of software vulnerabilities goes unnoticed, as attackers did not find anything meaningful or they stole something where software creators have no idea.

This section talks about these security practices which we should implement in our programming and coding life.

"Secure Coding: It's Better to Be Safe Than Sorry"

What is Secure Coding?

Secure coding standards govern the coding practices, techniques, and decisions that developers make while building software. They aim to ensure that developers write code that minimizes security vulnerabilities. Development tasks can typically be solved in many different ways, with varying levels of complexity. Some solutions are more secure than others, and secure coding standards encourage developers and software engineers to take the safest approach, even if it is not the fastest.

For example, secure coding best practices often

mandate a “default deny” approach to access permissions. Developers using secure coding techniques create code that denies access to sensitive resources unless an individual can demonstrate that they are authorized to access it.

There are several secure coding standards and coding security guides in widespread use today, including the OWASP Secure Coding Practices and the SEI CERT Coding Standards.

Why Should You Use Secure Coding Standards?

In the 2017 breach at Equifax, malicious individuals accessed personal information because of compromised software at the foundation of their organization. That isn’t the first organization, or the last, to find holes in its secure coding practices and leave themselves open to exploitation.

According to a 2019 survey completed by Sonatype, one in four companies confirmed or suspected a web application breach related to open source components. That number is staggering when you consider the odds that your organization will be next to experience a breach if you don't initiate coding security best practices.

How to Ensure Your Code is Secure

By patching your systems regularly, you're taking these secure coding guidelines to the next level. Patch and vulnerability management is focused on identifying risk and enabling systems to stay up to date. Through these methods and security testing, you're ensuring that your code is properly checked for errors.

Best Practices for Secure Coding

Secure coding is a group of best practices that'll enable you to secure your code as you go. In this article, we've selected for you the most important ones. And, as brevity is the soul of wit, we've also summarized them in one handy table.

Coding Practice	How to Implement It
1. Input validation: Never Trust User Input	✓ Check data length ✓ Validate characters set ✓ Check data format ✓ Use restrictions
2. Manage Authentication and Passwords	✓ Use transport layer security (TLS) client authentication ✓ Implement authentication error messages ✓ Store, control and manage your passwords safely ✓ Transmits passwords securely

3. Sanitize Data First, Then Send the Inputs to Other Systems

- ✓ Use a whitelist (allowlist)
- ✓ Use a blacklist (blocklist)
- ✓ Escape inputs to keep things safe

4. Adopt the Principle of Least Privilege

- ✓ Validate permissions on every request
- ✓ Create tests to validate permissions before release
- ✓ Periodically review permissions

5. Architecture: Make It Unique and Secure

- ✓ Use subsystems
- ✓ Follow OWASP' secure architecture (SA) practice
- ✓ Load only secure plugins and libraries

6. Keep It Intuitive But Effective

- ✓ Use a simple and small design
- ✓ Don't over-complicate your security controls
- ✓ Be user-friendly

7. Deny Access by Default

- ✓ Keep unauthenticated users out
- ✓ Apply this policy to new user accounts too
- ✓ Keep new features sealed

8. Go Deep With Your Defense: Create Multiple Security Layers

- ✓ Configure the security settings of each application
- ✓ Pair secure programming with secure runtime environments
- ✓ Don't forget authentication checkers

9. Secure Your Work and Communication

- ✓ Use strong, readily available encryption
- ✓ Protect your database
- ✓ Use trusted security certificates
- ✓ Sign your code before releasing it

10. Check the Quality of Your Code and Follow Coding Standards

- ✓ Review your code
- ✓ Use effective quality assurance mechanisms
- ✓ Use coding standards developed by international bodies
- ✓ Prevent attacks with threat modeling

Identifying Common Security Vulnerabilities

Identifying common security vulnerabilities is crucial for developing secure software applications. Here are some of the most prevalent security vulnerabilities to watch out for:

1. **Injection Attacks:**
   - SQL Injection (SQLi): Attackers inject malicious SQL queries through user inputs, potentially gaining unauthorized access to a database.
   - Cross-Site Scripting (XSS): Malicious scripts are injected into web pages viewed by other users, compromising their data or session.

2. **Authentication and Session Management:**
   - Broken Authentication: Weak or ineffective authentication mechanisms can lead to unauthorized access.
   - Session Fixation: Attackers set session identifiers, potentially allowing them to hijack

a user's session.

3. **Insecure Deserialization:**
   - Data deserialization vulnerabilities can lead to remote code execution or data tampering if not properly validated.

4. **Sensitive Data Exposure:**
   - Failing to protect sensitive data, like passwords or credit card numbers, can result in data breaches.

5. **XML External Entity (XXE) Injection:**
   - Attackers can exploit XML processors to disclose internal files, execute remote requests, or perform denial-of-service attacks.

6. **Broken Access Control:**
   - Inadequate access controls may allow users to access unauthorized resources or perform actions they shouldn't.

7. **Security Misconfigurations:**
   - Improperly configured security settings, such

as open ports or default credentials, can expose vulnerabilities.

8. **Cross-Site Request Forgery (CSRF):**
   - Malicious websites trick users into executing unwanted actions on a different site where they are authenticated.

9. **Using Components with Known Vulnerabilities:**
   - Outdated or vulnerable software components, libraries, or frameworks can introduce security risks.

10. **Unvalidated Redirects and Forwards:**
    - Attackers may redirect users to malicious websites or perform phishing attacks through unvalidated redirects.

11. **API Security Issues:**
    - Poorly secured APIs can expose sensitive data or allow unauthorized access.

12. **Insufficient Logging and Monitoring:**

- Inadequate logging and monitoring make it challenging to detect and respond to security incidents.

13. **Elevation of Privilege:**
    - Vulnerabilities that allow attackers to escalate their privileges within an application or system.

14. **Security Through Obscurity:**
    - Relying solely on the secrecy of algorithms, keys, or methods as a security measure is risky.

15. **Inadequate Rate Limiting and Resource Exhaustion:**
    - Lack of rate limiting can lead to abuse, resource exhaustion, or denial-of-service attacks.

16. **Content Spoofing and Phishing:**
    - Attackers may manipulate content or URLs to deceive users or steal sensitive information.

17. **Denial-of-Service (DoS) Attacks:**

- Attackers flood an application or system with traffic to overwhelm and disrupt its normal functioning.

Identifying and addressing these common security vulnerabilities requires a combination of secure coding practices, regular security testing, vulnerability assessments, and a strong security mindset throughout the software development lifecycle.

Automating Code Reviews for Security

Automating code reviews for security is a critical practice in the DevSecOps pipeline to identify and address vulnerabilities early in the software development process. Here's a detailed explanation of how to set up and automate code reviews for security:

1. **Choose a Static Analysis Tool:**
   - Start by selecting a static code analysis tool suitable for your programming language and technology stack. Popular options include OWASP Dependency-Check, SonarQube, Checkmarx, and Fortify.

2. **Integration with CI/CD Pipeline:**

- Integrate the chosen static analysis tool into your CI/CD pipeline. This ensures that every code change triggers an automated security scan before code is merged or deployed.
- Configure the tool to provide scan results in a format compatible with your CI/CD platform (e.g., JUnit XML or JSON).

3. **Establish Baseline Rules:**
   - Define a set of baseline security rules and coding standards that align with your organization's security policies and industry best practices. These rules will be used by the static analysis tool to identify security issues.
   - Customize the ruleset to exclude or include specific checks based on your application's requirements.

4. **Continuous Monitoring:**
   - Enable continuous monitoring of the codebase by scheduling regular scans. This ensures that newly introduced vulnerabilities are promptly detected.
   - Set up alerts and notifications to inform

developers and security teams of security findings.

5. **Quality Gates and Break Builds:**
    - Implement quality gates as part of your CI/CD pipeline. If the static analysis tool identifies critical security vulnerabilities, consider breaking the build or blocking deployment until the issues are resolved.
    - Define thresholds for acceptable levels of risk based on your organization's risk tolerance.

6. **Contextual Analysis:**
    - Ensure that the static analysis tool provides contextual analysis to reduce false positives. Tools that understand the context of your codebase are more accurate in identifying real security issues.
    - Use taint analysis to trace data flow and identify potential security vulnerabilities accurately.

7. **Remediation Workflow:**

- Implement a remediation workflow that allows developers to review and address identified vulnerabilities. This may include creating issues or tickets in your issue tracking system (e.g., Jira) and assigning them to the responsible developers.

- Encourage developers to provide information on how they remediated each vulnerability to promote knowledge sharing.

8. **Training and Awareness**:

   - Provide training and awareness programs to educate developers about common security issues and best practices. This empowers them to write more secure code and understand the importance of the automated code review process.

9. **Trend Analysis and Reporting:**

   - Analyze trends in security findings over time to identify recurring issues or areas of improvement. Regularly review and update your baseline rules to adapt to evolving threats.

- Generate comprehensive reports on security findings and share them with stakeholders, including developers, security teams, and management.

10. **Continuous Improvement: -**

Continuously evaluate the effectiveness of your automated code review process. Collect feedback from developers and security teams to identify areas for improvement. - Consider adding dynamic analysis (DAST) and interactive application security testing (IAST) to complement static analysis for a more comprehensive security assessment.

Automating code reviews for security not only helps in identifying and addressing vulnerabilities early but also fosters a culture of security within your development team. It is an essential component of DevSecOps, enabling secure and efficient software delivery.

CHAPTER 4

Vulnerability Management and Patching

This chapter delves deep into the essential aspects of identifying, prioritizing, and addressing vulnerabilities within your DevOps environment. In our summary, let's take a look at what lies ahead:

The Importance of Vulnerability Management in DevOps:

- Understand why vulnerability management is indispensable in DevOps.
- Learn how it goes beyond mere threat detection to proactive risk mitigation.
- Explore how a robust vulnerability management

process can prevent costly security breaches.

Scanning for Vulnerabilities in Dependencies and Libraries:

- Discover the significance of scanning third-party dependencies and libraries.
- Learn how to employ tools and techniques to identify vulnerabilities.
- Understand why staying up-to-date with security patches is crucial.

Prioritizing and Remediating Vulnerabilities:

- Learn the art of prioritizing vulnerabilities based on their severity and impact.
- Explore strategies to remediate vulnerabilities efficiently.
- Understand the role of risk-based prioritization in optimizing your security efforts.

Automated Patch Management Strategies:

- Uncover the benefits of automated patch management in DevOps.
- Learn how to implement patch management systems effectively.

- Explore best practices for automating the patching process without disrupting operations.

In the subsequent sections of this chapter, we'll deep dive into each of these topics, providing you with practical insights, real-world examples, and strategies to effectively manage vulnerabilities and apply patches within your DevOps workflow.

Vulnerability management and patching are integral to the continuous security posture of any DevOps environment. By the end of this chapter, you'll be well-equipped to proactively address vulnerabilities, enhance your system's security, and maintain a robust and resilient DevOps pipeline. So, let's dive in and harness the power of vulnerability management and patching in DevOps.

The Importance of Vulnerability Management in DevOps

In today's digital landscape, where cyber threats are increasingly sophisticated and prevalent, the importance of vulnerability management within DevOps cannot be overstated. Vulnerability management is the proactive practice of identifying, assessing, prioritizing, and mitigating security vulnerabilities in software, systems, and infrastructure. It's not just a security concern; it's a

DevOps imperative.

Why is Vulnerability Management Critical in DevOps?

Question 1: Why should DevOps teams prioritize vulnerability management?

DevOps promotes agility and continuous delivery, enabling organizations to release software faster than ever before. However, this agility can inadvertently introduce vulnerabilities. Vulnerability management in DevOps ensures that security is integrated into this rapid pace of development. By proactively identifying and addressing vulnerabilities, teams can mitigate risks and maintain the integrity of their systems.

Case Study 1: The Equifax Data Breach

In 2017, Equifax, one of the three major credit-reporting agencies, suffered a massive data breach that exposed sensitive information of nearly 143 million people. The breach was attributed to a known vulnerability in Apache Struts that had not been patched. This incident underscores the criticality of vulnerability management. Equifax's failure to patch a known vulnerability resulted in one of the most significant data breaches in history.

Question 2: How does vulnerability management align with DevOps principles?

"Vulnerability management aligns perfectly with DevOps principles such as collaboration, automation, and continuous improvement. By involving all stakeholders, automating vulnerability scans, and continuously refining security measures, DevOps teams can maintain a secure and agile development environment."

Case Study 2: Netflix's Simian Army

Netflix, a pioneer in DevOps practices, created the Simian Army, a suite of tools designed to intentionally introduce failures and vulnerabilities into their systems. This practice, known as Chaos Engineering, allows Netflix to proactively identify weaknesses and vulnerabilities in their infrastructure. It's a testament to how vulnerability management can be integrated into DevOps culture.

Neglecting vulnerability management in DevOps can have severe consequences. It exposes organizations to security breaches, data loss, legal and regulatory issues, and damage to their reputation. Additionally, the cost of addressing vulnerabilities post-release is often much higher than addressing them during development.

Case Study 3: The WannaCry Ransomware Attack

The WannaCry ransomware attack in 2017 impacted organizations worldwide. It exploited a vulnerability in Microsoft Windows for which a security patch had been available for months. The attack affected hospitals, businesses, and government agencies. Had vulnerability management been diligently practiced, this widespread attack could have been prevented.

Vulnerability management should be integrated into every phase of the DevOps lifecycle. This includes:

- **Design**: Ensuring secure architecture and threat modeling.
- **Development**: Writing secure code and conducting code reviews.
- **Testing**: Performing vulnerability scanning and

security testing.

- **Deployment**: Automating security checks in the deployment pipeline.
- **Monitoring**: Continuously monitoring for new vulnerabilities and threats in production.

Case Study 4: Jenkins and OWASP Dependency-Check

Jenkins, a popular DevOps automation server, integrates with tools like OWASP Dependency-Check, which automatically scans project dependencies for known vulnerabilities. By doing so, Jenkins users can identify and address vulnerabilities at the development and build stages, seamlessly integrating vulnerability management into the DevOps pipeline.

In summary, vulnerability management in DevOps is not just a practice; it's a necessity. It aligns with DevOps principles, reduces security risks, and ultimately enables organizations to release software more securely and confidently. As we delve deeper into this chapter, we'll explore strategies for scanning and prioritizing vulnerabilities, as well as best practices for remediation and automated patch management.

Scanning for Vulnerabilities in Dependencies and Libraries

One of the fundamental challenges in modern software development is managing the multitude of third-party dependencies and libraries that applications rely on. While these components can accelerate development, they can also introduce vulnerabilities if not carefully managed. This is where scanning for vulnerabilities in dependencies and libraries becomes crucial.

Identifying Vulnerabilities in Third-Party Code

Consider this scenario: You're building a web application, and to save time, you decide to use a popular open-source library for user authentication. This library is widely trusted and used by many developers. However, a few weeks into development, you receive a security advisory that the library you're using contains a critical vulnerability. What do you do?

The Heartbleed Bug

In 2014, the Heartbleed bug rocked the cybersecurity world. It was a vulnerability in the widely used OpenSSL library, which is responsible for securing communication over the internet. Heartbleed allowed attackers to read sensitive data from the memory of the affected server. The incident highlighted the importance of scanning for vulnerabilities in widely adopted libraries.

Why is it crucial to scan third-party dependencies for vulnerabilities?

Third-party dependencies, especially widely used ones, can have a broad impact if they contain vulnerabilities. Scanning for vulnerabilities helps you identify and address these issues before they can be exploited, safeguarding your application's security.

Tools for Dependency Scanning

To scan for vulnerabilities in dependencies and libraries, you can turn to a variety of tools and services. These tools analyze your project's dependencies and cross-reference them with known vulnerability databases. They can provide reports detailing which dependencies have vulnerabilities and suggest updates or patches.

OWASP Dependency-Check

The OWASP Dependency-Check tool is a widely used open-source solution for identifying and monitoring known vulnerabilities in project dependencies. It integrates seamlessly with various build tools and CI/CD pipelines, making it a popular choice among DevOps teams.

Snyk

Snyk is another tool that specializes in identifying vulnerabilities in open-source libraries and container images. It offers continuous monitoring and automated fixes, streamlining the process of keeping your dependencies secure.

How can these tools be integrated into the DevOps pipeline?

These tools can be integrated into your DevOps

pipeline by running scans during the build or deployment process. This ensures that every change is checked for vulnerabilities, providing early feedback to developers and reducing the risk of shipping insecure code.

Prioritizing and Remediating Vulnerabilities

Not all vulnerabilities are created equal. Some pose a higher risk than others, and this is where prioritization becomes critical. Vulnerability scanning tools often provide severity ratings for each issue found, helping teams focus on the most urgent problems.

Common Vulnerability Scoring System (CVSS)

CVSS is a standardized system for assessing the severity of vulnerabilities. It assigns a score based on factors like the exploitability of the vulnerability and its potential impact. This scoring system aids in prioritizing vulnerabilities and allocating resources for remediation.

Why is prioritization important, and how does it impact the vulnerability management process?

Prioritization ensures that resources are allocated efficiently. It allows teams to address the most critical vulnerabilities first, reducing the overall risk to the organization. Without prioritization, teams may waste time on low-risk issues while high-risk vulnerabilities remain unaddressed.

In summary, scanning for vulnerabilities in dependencies and libraries is a fundamental practice for DevOps teams. It helps identify and prioritize vulnerabilities in third-party code, reducing the risk of security breaches. By integrating dependency scanning tools into the DevOps pipeline, teams can ensure that security is an integral part of the development process, rather than an afterthought.

Automated Patch Management Strategies

Managing vulnerabilities in software and systems is an ongoing process, and automated patch management is a cornerstone of this effort. Patch management is the systematic process of applying updates, known as patches, to software, applications, and systems to address vulnerabilities and improve security. Here, we explore the importance of automated patch management strategies in DevOps and how they contribute to a secure and agile development environment.

The Need for Automated Patch Management

In the fast-paced world of DevOps, rapid software development and continuous integration can introduce vulnerabilities. Automated patch management ensures that security updates are consistently applied to mitigate these risks.

Case Study: The WannaCry Ransomware Attack

The WannaCry ransomware attack in 2017 exploited a vulnerability in Windows for which a patch had been available months before the attack. Organizations that had automated patch management systems in place were able to swiftly apply the patch and protect their systems, while those without such systems were vulnerable.

Why is manual patch management insufficient in DevOps environments?

In DevOps, where changes are frequent and continuous, manual patch management can be slow and error-prone. Automated patch management ensures that patches are applied consistently and quickly, reducing the window of vulnerability.

Strategies for Automated Patch Management

- **Regular Scanning and Assessment:** Automated patch management starts with regular vulnerability scanning. Vulnerability scanning tools identify which patches are needed. These scans should be integrated into the DevOps pipeline.
- **Risk-Based Prioritization**: Not all patches are of equal importance. Prioritize patches based on risk to focus resources on the most critical vulnerabilities first. This aligns with DevOps principles of efficiency.
- **Test Environments**: Before deploying patches to production, test them in development and staging environments to ensure they don't introduce compatibility issues or disruptions.
- **Automated Deployment:** Once patches are validated, automate their deployment to production. This automation ensures consistency and reduces the risk of human error.
- **Rollback Mechanisms**: Have mechanisms in

place to rollback patches in case they cause unexpected issues in production. Automation should extend to rollback processes as well.

Example: Chef and Ansible for Configuration Management

Tools like Chef and Ansible can automate the configuration management process, including patch management. They allow you to define the desired state of your systems, ensuring that the necessary patches are applied consistently across all environments.

Question: What challenges might you face when implementing automated patch management in a DevOps environment, and how can they be overcome?

Challenges may include compatibility issues with existing systems, ensuring automated tests cover patched components, and coordinating patch deployment across multiple environments. Overcoming these challenges involves comprehensive testing, thorough planning, and gradual deployment strategies.

Continuous Monitoring and Feedback

Automated patch management is not a one-time task; it's an ongoing process. Continuous monitoring and feedback loops are essential to ensure that systems remain secure over time. Automated monitoring tools can detect new vulnerabilities and apply patches as soon as they become available.

Automated patch management is a critical component of DevOps security. It aligns with the DevOps principle of automation, allowing teams to maintain a secure environment without slowing down development processes. By implementing automated patch management strategies, organizations can proactively address vulnerabilities, reduce security risks, and enhance the overall security posture of their DevOps pipelines.

CHAPTER 5

Infrastructure as Code

In the ever-evolving landscape of DevOps and continuous security, infrastructure as code (IaC) emerges as a game-changer. IaC is a methodology that treats infrastructure provisioning, configuration, and management as code, enabling automation, scalability, and consistency. This chapter delves into the significance of IaC in modern DevOps practices and how it intersects with security.

Why Infrastructure as Code Matters in DevOps

Imagine having the ability to define and manage your infrastructure using the same version control, automation, and collaboration practices as your application code. This is precisely what IaC offers. By codifying infrastructure, teams can reap several benefits:

- **Automation**: IaC enables the automated provisioning and scaling of infrastructure, reducing manual interventions and potential errors.

- **Version Control:** Infrastructure configurations become versioned, allowing teams to track changes, collaborate, and roll back to previous states if issues arise.
- **Consistency**: IaC ensures that infrastructure remains consistent across various environments, from development and testing to production.
- **Scalability**: Scaling infrastructure up or down becomes a simple code change, aligning with the scalability demands of DevOps.

Security in Infrastructure as Code

Security is not an afterthought in IaC; it's an integral part of the process. By implementing security practices within your IaC workflows, you can ensure that security controls are consistently applied across your infrastructure.

In this chapter, we'll explore the world of Infrastructure as Code and its profound impact on DevOps and security. We'll delve into the principles of IaC, tools and frameworks, building reusable infrastructure components, managing IaC in different environments, and continuous compliance monitoring and auditing. By the end of this chapter, you'll have a deep understanding of how IaC can enhance security and agility in your DevOps journey.

Understanding Infrastructure as Code (IaC)

Infrastructure as Code (IaC) is a paradigm shift in the world of IT operations and infrastructure management. It treats infrastructure provisioning, configuration, and management as code, bringing automation, scalability, and consistency to the forefront. In this section, we'll explore what IaC is, why it matters, and provide examples and use cases that illustrate its significance.

What is Infrastructure as Code?

At its core, IaC is the practice of defining and managing infrastructure through code and automation scripts. Instead of manually configuring servers, networks, and other components, IaC allows you to describe your desired infrastructure in code. This code is versioned, stored in repositories, and can be executed to create, modify, or delete infrastructure resources.

Why Does IaC Matter?

- **Automation**: IaC enables automation of infrastructure provisioning and management tasks, reducing human error and saving time.
- **Consistency**: With IaC, you can ensure that your infrastructure remains consistent across different environments, from development and testing to production.
- **Version Control:** Infrastructure code is stored in version control systems (e.g., Git), allowing teams to track changes, collaborate, and roll back to previous configurations if issues arise.
- **Scalability**: Scaling infrastructure becomes a matter of modifying code, making it highly

adaptable to dynamic workload requirements.

IaC in Action: Examples and Use Cases

Example 1: Provisioning Virtual Machines

Consider a scenario where you need to provision virtual machines (VMs) for a web application. With IaC, you can define the VM configurations, including the number of VMs, size, networking, and operating system, in a code template. Using tools like Terraform or AWS CloudFormation, you can then execute this code to create and configure the VMs automatically.

Use Case 1: Continuous Integration and Continuous Deployment (CI/CD)

In a CI/CD pipeline, IaC is instrumental in creating and managing the infrastructure needed for automated testing and deployment. When a new version of your application is ready for testing or production, IaC scripts can spin up the necessary infrastructure, deploy the application, run tests, and tear down resources when testing is complete—all with code.

Example 2: Container Orchestration with Kubernetes

Kubernetes, a popular container orchestration platform, relies heavily on IaC principles. You define your desired containerized application architecture, including pods, services, and scaling policies, in Kubernetes configuration files (YAML). Kubernetes interprets these files as code, automating the deployment, scaling, and management of containers.

Use Case 2: Multi-Cloud Deployment

In a multi-cloud environment, IaC provides a consistent way to manage infrastructure across different cloud providers. You can use tools like HashiCorp Terraform to write IaC scripts that abstract the differences between clouds and deploy resources on AWS, Azure, and Google Cloud, for example, with the same codebase.

IaC empowers DevOps teams to automate infrastructure management, ensure consistency, and accelerate the software delivery pipeline. By treating infrastructure as code, organizations can achieve greater agility and efficiency while reducing the risk of manual configuration errors. Whether you're provisioning VMs, managing containers, or orchestrating multi-cloud deployments, IaC is a powerful approach that can revolutionize your DevOps practices.

Tools and Frameworks for IaC

Infrastructure as Code (IaC) is a fundamental practice in modern DevOps, enabling the automation and management of infrastructure through code. To implement IaC effectively, you can leverage a variety of tools and frameworks that simplify the process and provide powerful features for infrastructure provisioning and management. Here are some of the most widely used tools and frameworks for IaC:

1. **Terraform**:
   Terraform is an open-source IaC tool developed by HashiCorp. It allows you to define your infrastructure as code using a declarative configuration language. Terraform supports a wide range of cloud providers, including AWS, Azure, Google Cloud, and more. It enables you to create and manage infrastructure resources, such as virtual machines, networks, and databases, in a consistent and automated manner.

2. **AWS CloudFormation:**
   AWS CloudFormation is Amazon Web Services' native IaC service. It provides templates written in JSON or YAML to define and provision AWS resources. CloudFormation templates can describe entire environments, including EC2 instances, RDS databases, security groups, and more. This tool is particularly well-suited for AWS-centric infrastructures.

3. **Azure Resource Manager (ARM) Templates:** For Microsoft Azure users, Azure Resource Manager templates offer a way to define infrastructure as code. These templates are JSON files that describe Azure resources and their dependencies. With ARM templates, you can automate the provisioning and management of Azure services like virtual networks, storage accounts, and web apps.

4. **Google Cloud Deployment Manager:**

   Google Cloud's IaC solution, Deployment Manager, uses YAML or Jinja2 templates to define and deploy Google Cloud Platform resources. It provides a way to describe the entire environment, including VM instances, Cloud Storage buckets, and networking components, in code.

5. **Ansible**:

Ansible is a versatile automation tool that can be used for IaC. It uses simple YAML scripts called "playbooks" to describe the desired state of systems and infrastructure. Ansible is agentless, making it easy to use for configuration management, application deployment, and orchestration across various platforms.

6. **Puppet**:

   Puppet is a popular configuration management tool that also supports IaC practices. Puppet uses a declarative language to define infrastructure configurations and ensure systems are in the desired state. It is particularly useful for managing server configurations and application deployments.

7. **Chef**:

   Chef is another configuration management tool that can be used for IaC. It uses code-driven recipes and cookbooks to automate infrastructure provisioning and management tasks. Chef excels in configuring and maintaining complex systems.

8. **Pulumi**:

Pulumi is an IaC platform that allows you to write infrastructure code in your preferred programming language, including Python, JavaScript, and TypeScript. It supports multiple cloud providers and enables you to define infrastructure as code using familiar programming constructs.

9. **Kubernetes Operators:**

   In the world of container orchestration, Kubernetes Operators are a way to define and manage applications and services as code. Operators extend Kubernetes to automate complex operational tasks, making them a valuable tool for IaC in containerized environments.

These are just a few of the many tools and frameworks available for implementing Infrastructure as Code. The choice of tool depends on your specific requirements, existing infrastructure, and cloud provider preferences. When selecting an IaC tool, consider factors such as ease of use, community support, integration capabilities, and the level of abstraction it provides for your infrastructure management needs.

Building a Reusable Infrastructure Components

One of the key advantages of Infrastructure as Code

(IaC) is the ability to create reusable infrastructure components that can be easily replicated across projects and environments. This practice promotes consistency, reduces duplication of effort, and accelerates the provisioning of infrastructure resources. In this section, we'll explore how to build and leverage reusable infrastructure components effectively.

1. **Module-Based Approach:**

   To build reusable infrastructure components, adopt a module-based approach. Modules are self-contained units of code that encapsulate a specific piece of infrastructure. For example, you can create modules for virtual machines, databases, load balancers, and networking components. Each module should have well-defined inputs and outputs, making it versatile and easy to integrate into different projects.

2. **Parameters and Variables:**

   Use parameters and variables to make your modules configurable. Parameters allow users of the module to provide input values, such as instance sizes or resource names, when they use the module. Variables help you define values that can be reused within the module, enhancing its flexibility.

Example:

Let's say you're building a module for deploying virtual machines. You can define parameters for the instance type, operating system, and number of instances. Variables can be used for common settings like the region, AMI ID, and security groups.

```
Variable "region" {description = "AWS region
for the VM"default   = "us-east-1"}
```

```
variable "instance_type" {description =
"Instance type for the VM"}

variable "ami_id" {description = "AMI ID for
the VM"}

# Parameters
parameter "num_instances" {description =
"Number of VM instances to create"}

parameter "instance_tags" {description =
"Tags to apply to the VM instances" type =
map(string)}
```

3. **Documentation**:
   Thoroughly document your reusable modules to

make them user-friendly. Provide clear instructions on how to use the module, including required inputs, expected outputs, and any dependencies. Effective documentation encourages adoption and helps team members understand how to leverage the module correctly.

4. **Version Control:**
   Just like application code, infrastructure code should be versioned. Use version control systems like Git to manage your infrastructure code repositories. When changes or improvements are made to a reusable module, update its version, and ensure that existing projects can reference the desired module version.

5. **Testing and Validation:**
   Test your reusable modules rigorously to ensure they work as expected. Implement automated tests that validate the correctness of the module's behavior, especially if it's used across multiple projects. Continuous integration (CI) pipelines can be set up to run these tests automatically.

6. **Sharing and Collaboration:**

Encourage collaboration and sharing within your organization. Create a centralized repository or registry where reusable modules can be stored and accessed by various teams. This fosters collaboration and ensures that everyone benefits from shared infrastructure components.

Benefits of Reusable Infrastructure Components:

- **Consistency**: Reusable components ensure that infrastructure is consistently provisioned, reducing configuration drift.
- **Efficiency**: Teams can save time and effort by leveraging pre-built modules, allowing them to focus on application-specific configurations.
- **Standardization**: Enforce best practices and standards by encapsulating them in reusable modules.
- **Scalability**: As projects grow, you can easily scale infrastructure by reusing proven components.
- **Maintainability**: Updates and improvements to infrastructure can be made in one place (the module), reducing maintenance overhead.

By following these practices, you can create a library of reusable infrastructure components that empower your DevOps teams to provision and manage infrastructure efficiently and consistently, whether they are working on a small project or a large-scale application.

Managing Infrastructure as Code in Different Environments

Managing infrastructure as code (IaC) across various environments is a critical aspect of DevOps and software development. DevOps teams often need to deploy and manage infrastructure in multiple environments, such as development, testing, staging, and production. Here's how to effectively manage IaC in different environments:

1. **Environment Parameterization:**
   When writing IaC scripts, parameterize environmental variables such as resource names, sizes, and network configurations. Create separate parameter files or variables for each environment, allowing you to customize settings for development, testing, and production. This ensures that your IaC is flexible and can adapt to different environments.

```
# Development environment variablesvariable
"instance_type" {description = "Instance type for
the VM" default  = "t2.micro"}

# Production environment variables
variable "instance_type" {description = "Instance
type for the VM" default = "m5.large"}
```

2. **Environment-Specific Configuration:**
   Maintain separate configuration files or directories for each environment. These files should specify which modules and resources to deploy in each environment. For example, you might use a "dev.tfvars" file for development and a "prod.tfvars" file for production. This separation allows you to keep environment-specific configurations organized.

3. **Use Conditional Logic:**
   Leverage conditional statements within your IaC scripts to control resource provisioning based on the environment. For instance, you can use "if" statements to deploy additional debugging resources in development that wouldn't be

needed in production.

Example (Terraform):

```
resource "aws_instance" "example" {ami =
var.ami_id instance_type = var.instance_type

 # Conditionally create tags for development
environment tags = var.environment ==
"development" ? local.dev_tags : local.prod_tags}
```

4. **Environment-Specific Pipelines:** Create distinct CI/CD pipelines for deploying IaC to different environments. Each pipeline should trigger when changes are made to the corresponding environment's branch or repository. This ensures that code changes are tested and deployed to the appropriate environment.

5. **Infrastructure as Code Promotion**: Implement a promotion process for IaC code changes. For example, code changes can be initially deployed to a development environment for testing. After successful testing, the same code can be promoted to the testing, staging, and

eventually production environments. Automated deployment pipelines can facilitate this process.

6. **Infrastructure State Management**:
   Use infrastructure state management tools like Terraform's state files or AWS CloudFormation stacks to track the state of deployed resources in each environment. Separate state files or stacks should be maintained for each environment to prevent conflicts and ensure isolation.

7. **Environment-Specific Variables:**
   Store environment-specific variables, secrets, and credentials securely. Use environment-specific secret management solutions to ensure that sensitive information is only accessible to authorized users and services in each environment.

8. **Regular Testing and Validation**:
   Perform regular testing and validation in each environment to ensure that IaC deployments are successful and that resources are correctly configured. Automated testing and validation

should be part of your CI/CD pipelines.

9. **Documentation and Communication:**
   Document the specific configurations, dependencies, and procedures for each environment. Maintain clear communication within the team regarding changes and updates to IaC code in different environments.

10. **Continuous Monitoring:**
    Implement continuous monitoring and alerting for infrastructure resources in all environments. This ensures that you can detect and respond to issues promptly, regardless of the environment.

By following these best practices, DevOps teams can effectively manage infrastructure as code in different environments, ensuring that deployments are consistent, reliable, and tailored to the specific needs of each stage in the software development lifecycle.

Continuous Compliance Monitoring and Auditing

Continuous compliance monitoring and auditing with Infrastructure as Code (IaC) is like having a watchful guardian for your digital world. It ensures that your systems and applications always follow the rules, just like how a referee enforces the rules in a sports game. Here's how it works:

- **Setting the Rules:** You start by defining the rules, like the game's rules in sports. These rules are often related to security and privacy and are called compliance standards. Examples include "Keep data safe" or "Only certain people can access this."
- **Checking Compliance Automatically**: With IaC, we use smart tools to automatically check if everything is following the rules. Think of these

tools as referees. They continuously watch over your digital infrastructure, like your servers and databases.

- **Fixing Rule Breaks:** When a rule is broken, just like when a player makes a foul in a game, the tools can automatically try to fix it. For example, if someone accidentally makes a server public when it should be private, the tool can change it back to private.
- **Regular Game Checks (Audits):** Just as sports leagues regularly check if teams are playing fair, we do regular checks called audits. Audits make sure that the rules are being followed and that our compliance-monitoring tools are doing their job.
- **Keeping Score:** We keep records of all the rule checks and fixes. These records are like a scoreboard. They show that we are playing by the rules and can prove it to others, like bosses or auditors.
- **Learning the Rules:** It's important that everyone on your team knows the rules of the game. So, we train and educate our team members about compliance standards and how to follow them.

It's like teaching players the rules of the sport.

- **Using Smart Tools:** To make things easier, we use smart tools and systems to automate most of the work. These tools help us quickly find and fix rule breaks without needing to do everything manually.

In simpler terms, continuous compliance monitoring and auditing with IaC is like having a vigilant referee and a well-trained team to ensure that your digital systems and applications always play by the rules, keeping your data safe and secure.

Implementing Security Controls in Cloud Environments

Securing your cloud environment with Infrastructure as Code (IaC) is like setting up a fortress to protect your treasures. IaC allows you to build strong security defenses in the digital world, just as you would in a castle. Here's how it works:

1. **Building Digital Fortifications:**

   Imagine your cloud resources are like the walls, gates, and moats of a castle. IaC lets you define these digital fortifications using code. You can create rules and settings to keep your resources safe and control who can access them.

2. **Access Control Lists (ACLs) and Firewalls:**

   In your digital castle, you can set up guards and

security checkpoints. With IaC, you can create Access Control Lists (ACLs) and firewalls that decide who is allowed in and who gets stopped at the gate. It's like having guards who check everyone's identity before granting access.

3. **Encryption Shields**:
   To protect sensitive information, you can add encryption to your digital treasures. IaC helps you apply encryption to your data, making it unreadable to anyone who shouldn't have access. It's like locking your treasures in a magical box only you can open.

4. **Monitoring Watchtowers:**
   Just as watchtowers in a castle help keep an eye on the surroundings, IaC allows you to set up monitoring tools that watch for any unusual activity in your cloud environment. These tools raise the alarm if they spot anything suspicious, like a guard noticing an intruder.

5. **Security Patches and Updates:**
   In your digital world, software needs updates to

fix vulnerabilities. IaC helps you automatically apply these updates, like repairing cracks in the castle walls. This keeps your environment strong and secure.

6. **Intrusion Detection**:

   To catch invaders, you can deploy digital sentinels. IaC allows you to set up intrusion detection systems that alert you when someone tries to break in. It's like having invisible guards that sound the alarm.

7. **Identity Verification:**

   Just as a castle requires anyone entering to prove their identity, IaC helps you set up identity and access management. You control who has keys to your digital gates, and you can change access permissions as needed.

8. **Compliance Shields:**

   IaC helps you follow the rules and regulations, just like a castle must adhere to the kingdom's laws. You can define compliance standards in your code to ensure your digital castle meets all security requirements.

9. **Security Training:**
   Finally, everyone in your digital kingdom needs to understand security. IaC encourages educating your team on security best practices, like teaching soldiers how to defend the castle.

In simple terms, implementing security controls in cloud environments with IaC is like fortifying your digital castle with strong walls, vigilant guards, and powerful magic. It helps you keep your digital treasures safe from intruders and ensures that your cloud kingdom remains secure.

Leveraging Security-as-Code Principles

Imagine your security measures are like a powerful spellbook, and Security-as-Code (SaC) is the magical language that allows you to cast protective spells on your digital world. SaC means using code to weave security into every part of your software and infrastructure. Here's what it does:

- **Automated Spells:** SaC lets you write code that automatically casts security spells. Instead of manually setting up security each time, you code your defenses, making them repeatable and reliable.
- **Continuous Vigilance**: Just as guards keep watch 24/7, SaC tools constantly check for security issues. They detect threats and vulnerabilities in real-time, like magical sentinels guarding your digital realm.

- **Rapid Response:** SaC helps you respond swiftly to security challenges. When a threat is detected, your code can automatically counter it, like having instant protective spells at your command.
- **Consistency Across Realms:** SaC ensures that security is consistent across different parts of your digital kingdom, whether it's in the cloud, on servers, or in applications. This uniformity strengthens your defenses.
- **Enchanted Documentation:** SaC adds magic to your documentation. Security practices and policies are written in code, so there's no ambiguity. Everyone knows how to cast the right protective spells.
- **Collaborative Spellcasting**: Just as wizards collaborate on powerful spells, your team collaborates on SaC code. This means that security is a shared responsibility, with everyone contributing to the protective spells.
- **Securing the Source**: SaC helps protect your source code, making sure it remains secret and unaltered. It's like putting an enchantment on your code repository to keep it safe.

In essence, leveraging Security-as-Code principles is

like becoming a skilled wizard who uses code to weave powerful protective spells over your digital kingdom. It makes security an integral part of your digital world, ensuring constant vigilance and rapid responses to threats.

CHAPTER 6

Containerization and Orchestration

In this chapter, we dive deep into the world of containerization and orchestration, two game-changing technologies that have reshaped how we develop, deploy, and manage applications.

Containerization Simplifies Deployment: Imagine having the power to package your applications and their dependencies into a neat, portable box that runs consistently across various environments. Containers offer precisely that capability, making application deployment a breeze.

Kubernetes Reigns Supreme: We'll explore the reigning champion of container orchestration, Kubernetes. Known as K8s for short, it automates the complex tasks of deploying and managing containerized applications, providing scalability and fault tolerance.

Scalability Made Easy: Scaling your applications becomes a straightforward affair with containers and Kubernetes. Whether you're facing a sudden surge in user traffic or planning for future growth, these technologies have you covered.

Microservices Flourish: We'll also delve into how containerization and orchestration underpin the microservices revolution. Break your applications into smaller, manageable components, leading to agility, easier maintenance, and robustness.

Security Matters: With the rise of container adoption, security becomes a paramount concern. Learn about essential security practices, including Kubernetes Security Context and container scanning, to shield your applications from vulnerabilities.

Hybrid and Multi-Cloud Ready: Containerization and orchestration seamlessly extend your application's reach across diverse cloud environments, making hybrid and multi-cloud strategies both feasible and efficient.

Serverless Integration: Finally, we'll explore how containerization bridges the gap between traditional server-based applications and serverless computing, opening up new possibilities for resource-efficient application deployment.

As we navigate this chapter, keep in mind that mastering containerization and orchestration is a significant step towards achieving a modern, secure, and highly adaptable DevOps environment. Let's embark on this exciting journey together.

Introduction to Containers and Docker

In today's rapidly evolving world of DevOps and cloud-native development, understanding containers and Docker is like possessing a versatile toolbox for software packaging and deployment. In this chapter, we'll embark on a journey to demystify containers, Docker, and their pivotal role in modern application development.

Containers Unveiled:

Containers are like magic capsules that encapsulate your applications along with all the necessary libraries and dependencies. They provide a consistent and isolated environment that ensures your applications run the same way, regardless of where they are deployed.

Docker Takes the Stage:

Docker, often synonymous with containers, is the leading star of containerization. It simplifies the creation, distribution, and management of containers. With Docker, you can build, share, and run containers effortlessly, making it a go-to tool for DevOps professionals.

A Closer Look at Docker:

Let's take a closer look at Docker's core components:

- **Docker Engine:** This is the heart of Docker, responsible for building, running, and managing containers. Think of it as the magician behind the scenes.
- **Docker Image:** An image is like a blueprint for containers. It contains everything needed to run an application. We'll explore how to create and use these images.
- **Docker Container:** Containers are instances of Docker images. You can run multiple containers from the same image, each isolated and self-

sufficient.

Architectural Insight:

To illustrate, consider a simplified architectural diagram:

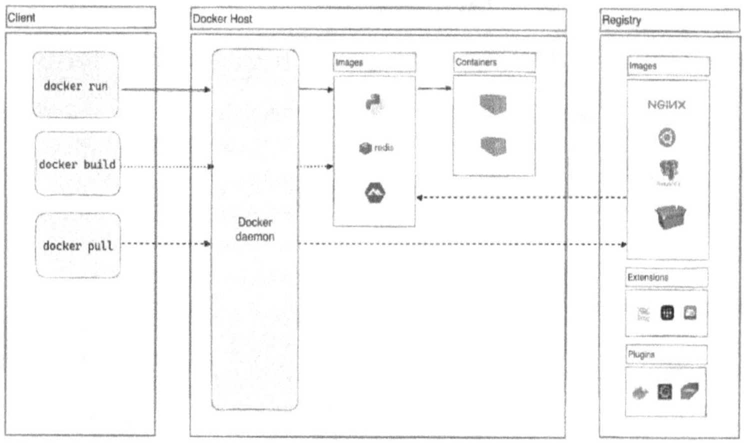

Imagine you have an application, and you want to run it on different servers or in the cloud. Instead of dealing with the complexities of configuring each server individually, you package your app into a Docker image. This image, along with the Docker Engine, ensures your app runs consistently, no matter where it's deployed.

Let's dive into real-world scenarios where Docker

shines:

- **Development Environments**: Developers can work on projects with all the required dependencies encapsulated in Docker containers, avoiding "it works on my machine" issues.
- **Microservices**: Docker's lightweight nature makes it ideal for microservices architectures. Each microservice can run in its own container, simplifying scaling and maintenance.
- **CI/CD Pipelines**: Docker is the go-to choice for building and deploying applications in continuous integration and continuous deployment (CI/CD) pipelines. It ensures that what's tested in one environment is the same as what's deployed in another.
- **Hybrid and Multi-Cloud**: Docker containers provide consistency in hybrid and multi-cloud deployments, allowing you to seamlessly move applications across cloud providers or on-premises infrastructure.

Throughout this chapter, we'll explore Docker's features, dive into hands-on examples, and witness how it revolutionizes application packaging and deployment. By the end, you'll have the tools and knowledge needed to leverage containers and Docker effectively in your DevOps journey

Container Orchestration with Kubernetes

Containerization has unlocked new possibilities for application deployment, but managing individual containers can quickly become a complex task. This is where Kubernetes, often referred to as K8s, emerges as the ultimate orchestrator, allowing you to tame the containerization beast and bring order to your deployment chaos.

Understanding Kubernetes:

Imagine Kubernetes as a conductor leading an orchestra. It manages and orchestrates your containers, ensuring they work together harmoniously. Here's what you need to know:

- **Nodes**: In the Kubernetes world, your servers are

called nodes. They can be physical servers or virtual machines. Nodes are the orchestra members, ready to play their part.

- **Pods**: Pods are like the smallest musical ensembles in our orchestra. They can contain one or more containers that work together as a unit. For example, a web application might have a container for the web server and another for the database.

- **Deployments**: Think of deployments as sheet music for your orchestra. They describe what the desired state of your application should be. Kubernetes ensures your application matches this desired state.

- **Services**: Services are like the audience in a concert hall. They provide a stable network address for accessing your application, no matter where it's running. This is essential for load balancing and scaling.

Basic Kubernetes Commands:

Let's get our hands dirty with some basic Kubernetes commands:

1. **Create a Deployment:** This command creates a deployment for your application.

   ```
   kubectl create deployment my-app --image=my-app-image:v1
   ```

2. **Scale Pods:** You can easily scale your application by adjusting the number of replicas.

   ```
   kubectl scale deployment my-app --replicas=3
   ```

3. **Exposing Services:** To expose your application to the outside world, you can create a service.

```
kubectl expose deployment my-app --
type=LoadBalancer --port=80
```

4. **Check Application Status:** You can check the status of your pods and deployments.

```
kubectl get pods
kubectl get deployments
```

Real-World Scenarios:

Kubernetes shines in various real-world scenarios:

- **Scaling**: Need more musicians in your orchestra? Kubernetes makes scaling as simple as adjusting the number of replicas in your deployment.
- **High Availability**: Kubernetes ensures that your application is highly available. If a pod (musician) fails, Kubernetes automatically replaces it to keep the show going.
- **Rolling Updates**: When it's time to update your application (change the sheet music), Kubernetes performs rolling updates without downtime.
- **Load Balancing**: Services act as your load

balancers, ensuring that traffic is evenly distributed among your pods.

- **Container Health**: Kubernetes constantly checks the health of your containers (musicians) and restarts them if they become unhealthy.
- **Multi-Cloud and Hybrid Cloud**: Kubernetes is cloud-agnostic, making it ideal for deploying applications across different cloud providers or on-premises environments.

Features and Best Practices for Deploying Large Cloud Applications with Kubernetes

Deploying large cloud applications with Kubernetes presents unique challenges and opportunities. To ensure success, consider the following features, best practices, and key considerations

1. **Horizontal Pod Autoscaling (HPA)**: For large applications, it's crucial to dynamically adjust the number of pods based on traffic. HPA automatically scales the number of pods in a deployment to maintain optimal performance, helping you manage unpredictable workloads

efficiently.

2. **Resource Requests and Limits**: Specify resource requests and **limits** for each pod to prevent resource contention. This ensures that pods have the necessary resources to run smoothly while preventing resource hogging.

3. **Node Affinity and Anti-Affinity:** Use node affinity and anti-affinity rules to control pod placement on specific nodes. This allows you to distribute pods strategically for optimal resource utilization and fault tolerance.

4. **Node Pools:** Divide your cluster into node pools with different **instance** types or configurations to accommodate varying workloads. For instance, you might have a node pool optimized for CPU-intensive tasks and another for memory-intensive workloads.

5. **Helm Charts**: Helm simplifies deploying, managing, and upgrading complex applications on Kubernetes. Create Helm **charts** for your large applications, making it easier to version and manage configurations.

6. **Network Policies**: Implement network policies to control **communication** between pods. Define rules that allow or deny traffic based on labels, protecting your application from unauthorized access and reducing attack surfaces.
7. **Rolling Updates with Canary Deployments:** Use rolling updates with canary deployments to minimize downtime during updates. Gradually roll out new versions of your application to a subset of users, monitor performance, and then proceed with the full deployment if everything looks good.

8. **StatefulSets**: For stateful components like databases, use StatefulSets to maintain stable network identities and storage volumes. This **ensures** data persistence and seamless pod replacement.

9. **Monitoring and Logging:** Implement robust monitoring and logging solutions to gain insights into the health and performance of your application. Tools like **Prometheus**, Grafana, and ELK Stack help detect issues early and optimize resource usage.

10. **Load Balancing:** Deploy a load balancer in front of your **application** to evenly distribute incoming traffic. Consider using Kubernetes-native services like Ingress controllers for routing and SSL termination.

11. **External Storage:** Utilize external storage solutions such as **Persistent** Volumes (PVs) and Persistent Volume Claims (PVCs) to manage data storage for your application. Ensure data persistence and availability, especially in stateful applications.

12. **CI/CD Pipelines**: Implement a robust CI/CD

pipeline to automate application testing and deployment. This ensures consistency and reliability in delivering updates to your large cloud application.

13. **Disaster Recovery**: Plan for disaster recovery by replicating data and workloads across multiple regions or **availability** zones. Kubernetes allows you to set up geo-distributed clusters for high availability.

14. **Cost Optimization**: Regularly review and optimize resource usage to control costs. Implement resource quotas, use cost management tools, and consider spot instances for non-critical workloads.

15. **Security**: Prioritize security by adhering to Kubernetes security best practices, regularly applying security **patches**, and conducting vulnerability assessments. Protect secrets and

sensitive data with secure storage solutions.

16. **Documentation**: Maintain detailed documentation for **your** Kubernetes configuration, deployment processes, and troubleshooting procedures. This knowledge sharing is invaluable for your team's success.

Large cloud applications on Kubernetes demand careful planning, **adherence** to best practices, and a deep understanding of the platform's features. By implementing these recommendations, you'll be well-equipped to deploy and manage robust, scalable, and resilient applications in the cloud.

Deploying and Scaling Applications with Containers

Deploying and scaling applications with containers

is a fundamental aspect of modern software development and infrastructure management. Containers provide a lightweight, portable, and consistent environment for running applications, while container orchestration platforms like Kubernetes enable efficient deployment and scaling. Let's dive into the details of how this process works:

1. **Containerization Basics:**
   - **Containers vs. Virtual Machines (VMs)**: Containers are similar to VMs but more lightweight. They share the host OS kernel, which makes them more efficient in terms of resource usage and faster to start compared to VMs.
   - **Packaging Applications:** Containers package an application along with its dependencies, libraries, and configurations into a single, portable unit. This ensures that the application runs consistently across different environments.
   - **Docker**: Docker is one of the most popular containerization platforms. It provides tools

for building, packaging, and distributing containers. Docker images serve as blueprints for containers.

2. **Deploying Containers**:
   - **Container Orchestration**: Deploying containers manually can be challenging, especially for complex applications. Container orchestration platforms like Kubernetes, Docker Swarm, and Amazon ECS automate the deployment and management of containers at scale.
   - **Pods**: In Kubernetes, the smallest deployable unit is a pod. A pod can contain one or more containers that share the same network namespace, storage, and configuration. Pods are the building blocks of your application.
   - **Deployments**: Deployments are used to manage the desired state of your application. They define the number of desired replicas (containers) and ensure that this desired state is maintained. Deployments support rolling updates and rollbacks.

3. **Scaling Containers**:
   - **Vertical Scaling (Scaling Up)**: You can vertically scale containers by increasing their resource limits (CPU, memory). However, this approach has limitations, and there's a threshold beyond which you can't scale further on a single machine.
   - **Horizontal Scaling (Scaling Out)**: Horizontal scaling involves adding more containers to handle increased load. Kubernetes supports automatic horizontal pod autoscaling (HPA) based on metrics like CPU utilization or custom metrics.

4. **Use Cases and Benefits:**
   - **Microservices**: Containers are well-suited for microservices architecture. Each microservice can run in its own container, providing isolation and scalability.
   - **CI/CD Pipelines**: Containers streamline the CI/CD process by ensuring that the development, testing, and production environments are consistent. This reduces the chances of "it works on my machine" issues.

- **Cost Efficiency:** Containers optimize resource usage by sharing the host OS kernel. This results in better resource utilization, reducing the number of servers needed and, consequently, infrastructure costs.
- **High Availability**: Containers can be distributed across multiple nodes in a cluster, ensuring high availability. If a node fails, containers can be rescheduled on healthy nodes.

5. **Challenges and Considerations**:

- **Resource Management**: Proper resource allocation and monitoring are crucial to avoid overcommitting or underutilizing resources.
- **Networking**: Managing network communication between containers and with external services requires careful planning and configuration.
- **Storage**: Containerized applications may require persistent storage, which must be handled effectively, especially in stateful applications.
- **Security**: Container security, including image

scanning, runtime protection, and access control, is critical to prevent vulnerabilities and breaches.

6. **Monitoring and Automation:**
   - **Monitoring**: Implement monitoring solutions like Prometheus and Grafana to track container and application performance, resource usage, and potential issues.
   - **Automation**: Leverage automation tools to deploy and manage containers, ensuring that scaling and updates are handled efficiently and consistently.

Kubernetes can do a lot of things for you. It can manage secrets, create load balancers, create and destroy cloud storages for your pods, and much more.

But at its core, the very point of Kubernetes is to manage deployments. I say "manage" because it's not only about running the deployments but also constantly checking if they're still running and are according to the specification.

Kubernetes is really good at that. It can automatically detect which node in your cluster is the best to run a deployment, and in case of a node failure, it'll automatically respawn your pod on another node.

Another feature of Kubernetes when it comes to deployments is scaling. It's possible to scale deployment up and down manually or automatically depending on different factors.

What Does It Mean to Scale a Deployment?

Let's get right on it. I assume you're here because you already have some deployment running on your Kubernetes cluster and want to scale it. What does it mean to "scale a deployment" on Kubernetes? It means changing the number of replicas for a deployment.

As you probably already know, when you create a deployment in Kubernetes, one of the parameters that you can **specify** in a spec section of a Kubernetes definition file is replicas. If you don't, by default, it'll take a value of 1. This means you'll get only one pod of your deployment running.

And while in some cases that's OK, in general, one of the main points of Kubernetes is to run highly available microservices. Therefore, you usually want to run more than one pod.

So, let's assume that you created a deployment without specifying replicas count, and so you have only one running pod for your deployment. You want to make your pod more resilient to node failures. Therefore, you decide to run four pods for that deployment instead.

You could simply find the YAML definition of your deployment, edit it to add a replicas parameter with a value of 4, and reapply the deployment from a file. But you can also change the replicas count for a running deployment directly on the cluster. That's where scaling a deployment comes into play.

Kubectl Scale

The easiest way to scale deployment is to use the **kubectl scale** command followed by a deployment you want to scale and desired replicas count after the –replicas parameter. So, for example, if you want to scale a deployment called "example-app," you can execute:

```
kubectl scale deployment/example-app --replicas=4
```

That's it. Now your deployment will be scaled up from one to four replicas. You can execute that command as many times as you'd like. Kubernetes will create more pods every time or delete some pods if you decide to scale down the deployment. Let's see that in action.

Our deployment is running now with four replicas, as per our scale action above.

Scaling to Zero

Guess what happens if you try to scale deployment to zero replicas. You'll see an error message? No, actually. Kubernetes will just patiently execute your request and delete all the pods for your deployment.

```
$ kubectl scale deployment/example-app --
replicas=0 deployment.apps/example-app scaled
$ kubectl get deployments
NAME READY  UP-TO-DATE AVAILABLE AGE
example-app  0/0 0 0 3m24s
```

What does this mean? Scaling deployment to zero effectively means disabling the deployment. It's disabling, not deleting, because the deployment object will still exist, as you can see in the code snippet above. It just doesn't have any running pods.

In fact, it's a common approach if you temporarily don't need that deployment. If you know that you'll need that deployment again soon, instead of deleting it and applying again later, you can scale it to zero and then scale it back to the desired amount later.

Not only is this approach a little bit faster than

deleting and re-creating the whole deployment, but it also gives you the added benefit of easily seeing the history of changes to the deployment. If you execute the following,

```
kubectl describe deployment example-app
```

at the bottom of the output, you'll see the list of all previous scaling actions

```
(...)
Events:

| Type   | Reason | Age | From | Message
|--------|-----------------|-------|--------------------|----
-------------------------------------------|
| Normal | ScalingReplicaSet | 11m   | deployment-controller | Scaled up replica set example-app-9456bbbf9 to 1   |
| Normal | ScalingReplicaSet | 10m   | deployment-controller | Scaled up replica set example-app-9456bbbf9 to 4   |
```

| Normal | ScalingReplicaSet | 9m7s | deployment-controller | Scaled down replica set example-app-9456bbbf9 to 2 |
| Normal | ScalingReplicaSet | 7m58s | deployment-controller | Scaled down replica set example-app-9456bbbf9 to 0 |

Scaling to 10,000

We know now what will happen if you scale to zero. Now, let's go the other way.

What happens if you try to scale to a very large number?

Well, it depends. If you have a very large cluster and the desired number of replicas can all fit on the nodes, then Kubernetes will simply scale as requested. However, if you have a small cluster and you try to scale, let's say, to 10,000 replicas, one of two things will happen.

Most likely, your scaling action will just stop at a certain number of pods.

```
NAME                READY       UP-TO-DATE      AVAILABLE     AGE
example-app         954/10000   954             954           4m42s
```

Kubernetes simply won't be able to fit more pods on your cluster, so it'll deploy as many as possible and then wait for more resources. This usually means either some other deployment being scaled down or adding more nodes to the cluster.

In a less optimistic but very possible scenario, your cluster will become very slow and eventually just overload itself and stop responding.

```
$ kubectl get deployments
Unable to connect to the server: net/http: TLS
handshake timeout
```

This can happen for the same reason as explained above. Your cluster will keep trying to deploy

10,000 pods but it can't, so it'll start constantly sending messages to nodes to check their available resources, and if the number of replicas you requested is way too high, it can lead to a DoS situation

Kubernetes comes with something called HorizontalPodAutoscaler

Automated Scaling

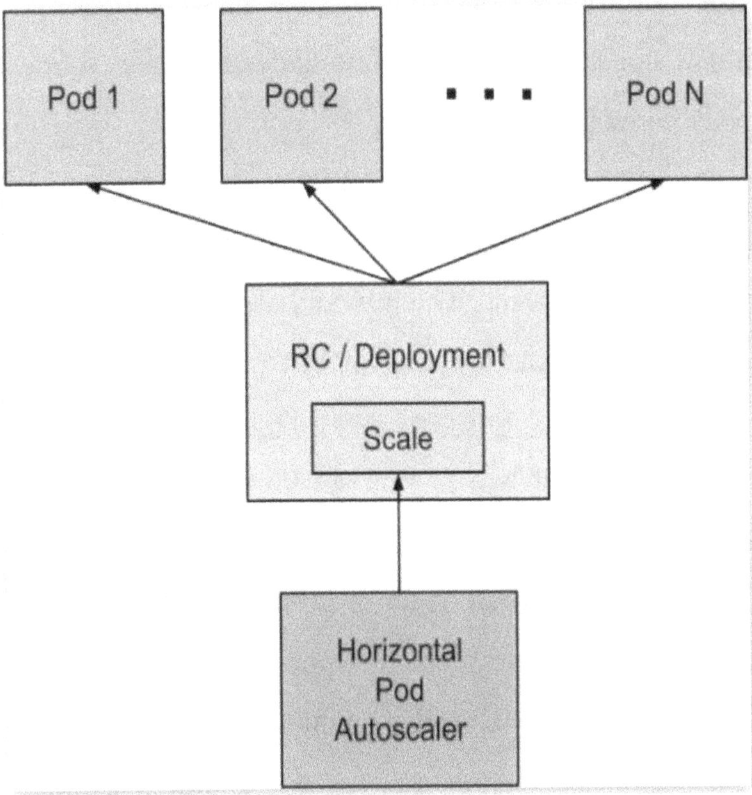

Now you know how to scale a deployment manually. Scaling deployments manually using the kubectl scale can be useful, but you don't want to manually scale the deployment every time there is, for example, a spike in traffic on your application.

In most situations, automated scaling can do the job for you. Kubernetes comes with something called

HorizontalPodAutoscaler. As the name suggests, it's a construct that can automatically scale your pods horizontally.

Horizontally means deploying more pods. There's also vertical scaling, which would assign more CPU and memory quota for pods instead.

So, how does it work? You set up Horizontal Pod Auto scaler once, and it'll then monitor your deployment and scale it up or down based on some metric. That metric most commonly will be a CPU usage of a pod. However, you can also instruct Horizontal Pod Auto scaler to monitor custom metrics from your application. To create a Horizontal Pod Auto scaler, you can use the **kubectl autoscale** command.

Let's see an example.

```
$ kubectl autoscale deployment example-app --cpu-
percent=80 --min=1 --max=10
horizontalpodautoscaler.autoscaling/example-app
autoscaled
```

In the command above, we instructed Kubernetes to monitor the CPU usage of our example-app deployment and to create new pods every time the average CPU usage for our deployment rises above 80%. You can get details of HorizontalPodAutoscaler by executing **kubectl get hpa**.

```
$ kubectl get hpa
NAME REFERENCE TARGETS MINPODS
MAXPODS REPLICAS AGE
example-app Deployment/example-app 2%/80% 1
10 1 3m3s
```

You can see that we currently have very low CPU usage for our deployment. Therefore, there's only one replica running. But if the load increases, our HPA should detect that.

```
$ kubectl get hpa
NAME REFERENCE TARGETS MINPODS
MAXPODS REPLICAS AGE
example-app Deployment/example-app   98%/80% 1
10 1 3m42s
```

And shortly after that, it should increase the number of pods to bring down the average CPU usage back below 80%.

```
$ kubectl get hpa
NAME REFERENCE  TARGETS MINPODS
MAXPODS REPLICAS AGE
example-app Deployment/example-app   53%/80% 1
10 4 4m11s
```

The HPA Algorithm

The controller uses a ratio between current and desired metric values to enable scaling. A typical calculation for desired replicas looks similar to:

```
desiredReplicas = ceil[currentReplicas * ( 
currentMetricValue / desiredMetricValue )]
```

This implies that if the current resource metric is 100m and the desired value is 50m, the number of replicas is calculated to be doubled (100/50=2).

Metrics Used by the HPA Object

The HPA object tracks two kinds of metrics:

Resource Metrics Resource metrics refers to the standard **resource management data**, such as memory and CPU consumption metrics, provided by the Kubernetes metric server.

Custom Metrics The HPA metrics interface also accepts custom metrics associated with a Kubernetes object through an API. The **custom metrics API** allows cluster administrators to install a metrics collector, collect the desired application metrics and expose them to the Kubernetes metrics server. Some commonly used custom metrics for Kubernetes include **request throughput**, **latency**,

dependencies, and **queue depth**.

Best Practices for Scaling Kubernetes Workloads

Some of the recommended practices for seamless workload scaling include:

Use an Up-To-Date Version of the Autoscaler Object

Kubernetes is a high-velocity platform with periodic addition of new features and releases. With every new release, performance and compatibility of different Kubernetes versions with the autoscaler releases are thoroughly tested and documented. It's recommended to use only the compatible autoscaling object of the Kubernetes control plane version to ensure the cluster autoscaler appropriately simulates the Kubernetes scheduler.

Keep Requests Close to the Actual Usage

The cluster autoscaler performs scaling operations depending on **node utilization** and **pending pods**. If pod resources are overprovisioned, workloads fail to either consume them efficiently or lead to lower node utilization. As the performance of a cluster's autoscaler is dependent on the resources provisioned for each pod, it's crucial to ensure the pod resource requests are **comparable to their actual consumption**. As a recommended best practice, cluster administrators leverage historical consumption statistics, and ensure each pod is allowed to request resources close to the actual trend of usage.

Node Groups Instances with Similar Capacity

A cluster autoscaler works with the assumption that every node of a node group has the same memory and CPU resource capacity. To achieve this, a template node is created by the autoscaler on which all cluster-wide scaling operations are performed. To ensure the autoscaler's created template node performs accurately, it's ideal to have node groups with nodes having the same resource footprint.

Define Resource Requests and Limits for Each Pod

The autoscaler relies on each node utilization and

pod scheduling status to tackle scaling changes. Calculating node utilization relies on a simple formula: dividing the sum of all the resources requested by the capacity of the node.

As a result, missing resource requests for one (or many) pod affects calculation of node utilization, thereby leading to suboptimal functioning of the algorithm. It's a recommended practice to ensure all pods running within a node have **resource requests and limits defined** for optimal scaling at any given time.

Specify Disruption Budgets for All Pods Kubernetes supports defining a pod disruption budget as a cluster object for voluntary/involuntary disruption of workload replicas to prevent incurring losses. Cluster administrators should define pod disruption budgets to ensure the autoscaler maintains a minimum threshold of pods for optimum functioning of cluster services while preventing budget overrun.

Best Practices for Container Security and Monitoring

In the world of containerization and Kubernetes, security and monitoring are paramount. Ensuring the safety of your applications and infrastructure, as well as gaining insights into their performance, requires a strategic approach. Let's explore best practices for container security and monitoring:

Container Security Best Practices:

- **Image Scanning**: Use image scanning tools to identify vulnerabilities in container images before deployment. These tools analyze images for known security issues and provide actionable insights for remediation.

- **Minimal Base Images**: Start with minimal base images like Alpine Linux. These images have fewer potential vulnerabilities, reducing your attack surface.
- **Regular Updates**: Keep container images and the underlying OS up to date with security patches. Implement a process for monitoring and applying updates promptly.
- **Least Privilege Principle**: Follow the principle of least privilege for container permissions. Containers should run with the minimum necessary permissions and capabilities.
- **Resource Constraints:** Limit resource consumption for containers using resource quotas and limits. This prevents resource abuse and helps maintain cluster stability.
- **Network Segmentation**: Implement network policies to control traffic between pods. Restrict communication to only what's necessary, reducing exposure to attacks.
- **Secret Management:** Use dedicated tools and best practices for managing secrets, such as

Kubernetes Secrets or external solutions like HashiCorp Vault

- **Runtime Protection**: Employ runtime security solutions that monitor containers for suspicious activities and enforce runtime policies.
- **Security Auditing**: Regularly audit container configurations and security policies to ensure compliance with best practices and organization-specific requirements.

Container Monitoring Best Practices:

- **Comprehensive Logging:** Implement centralized logging for containers and applications. Tools like Elasticsearch, Fluentd, and Kibana (EFK) or the ELK Stack enable effective log management.
- **Real-Time Metrics**: Collect real-time metrics from containers and applications to monitor performance. Prometheus is a popular choice for metric collection and alerting.
- **Alerting and Notifications:** Set up alerting rules based on predefined thresholds or anomaly

detection. Alert notifications should be sent to relevant team members for rapid response.

- **Tracing and Observability**: Utilize distributed tracing tools like Jaeger or Zipkin to gain insights into application performance and troubleshoot issues.
- **Resource Utilization Metrics**: Monitor CPU, memory, and disk usage to ensure efficient resource allocation and prevent resource bottlenecks.

- **Service Dependency Mapping**: Create visual representations of service dependencies to understand how different components of your application interact.
- **Auto-Scaling and Load Balancing**: Implement auto-scaling based on custom metrics or thresholds to ensure optimal resource usage during traffic spikes.
- **Long-Term Storage**: Archive historical monitoring data for analysis, compliance, and trend analysis. Consider solutions like InfluxDB

for long-term data storage.

- **Custom Dashboards:** Create custom dashboards that provide a clear overview of your application's health and performance, tailored to your specific needs.

Integrated Security and Monitoring:

Integrating security and monitoring practices is essential. For example, security incidents detected through monitoring can trigger automated responses, and monitoring data can be used to assess the impact of security measures.

By following these best practices, you'll establish a strong foundation for container security and monitoring. Your applications will be better protected against threats, and you'll have the visibility needed to maintain optimal performance and respond effectively to issues. Remember that security and monitoring are ongoing processes, requiring continuous assessment and improvement.

CHAPTER 7

Continuous Integration and Deployment

In this chapter, we delve into the essential practices of Continuous Integration and Continuous Deployment (CI/CD). These practices revolutionize software development by automating and streamlining the building, testing, and deployment of applications. Here's what we'll cover:

- **Introduction to CI/CD**: We begin by introducing the core concepts of CI/CD, explaining how it fosters collaboration among development and operations teams, accelerates software delivery, and improves the quality of applications.

- **Building an Effective CI Pipeline**: You'll learn how to set up a robust CI pipeline, which automates the process of compiling code, running tests, and producing deployable artifacts. We'll explore best practices for creating efficient CI workflows.
- **Automated Testing and Quality Assurance:** Discover the significance of automated testing in CI/CD. We'll cover various types of automated tests, including unit tests, integration tests, and end-to-end tests, and discuss how they contribute to application quality.
- **Integrating Static Code Analysis:** Learn how to integrate static code analysis tools into your CI/CD pipeline. We'll demonstrate how these tools identify code quality issues, security vulnerabilities, and maintainability concerns early in the development process.
- **Strategies for Continuous Deployment:** Explore strategies for automating the deployment of applications to production and staging environments. We'll discuss blue-green

deployments, canary releases, and feature flags, enabling you to roll out changes with confidence.

- **Continuous Monitoring and Feedback**: Understand the importance of monitoring in the CI/CD lifecycle. We'll cover real-time monitoring, alerting, and feedback loops, ensuring that you can promptly identify and respond to issues in production.
- **CI/CD Tools and Ecosystem**: Gain insights into popular CI/CD tools and platforms like Jenkins, Travis CI, GitLab CI/CD, and CircleCI. We'll also discuss cloud-native CI/CD solutions and the benefits they offer.
- **Best Practices and Pitfalls:** Discover best practices for designing effective CI/CD pipelines, along with common pitfalls to avoid. We'll provide guidance on structuring your CI/CD process for success.

By the end of this chapter, you'll have a comprehensive understanding of CI/CD principles, practical knowledge of setting up CI pipelines, and the ability to streamline the deployment of your applications with confidence and efficiency. CI/CD is a fundamental component of modern software development, enabling you to deliver high-quality software at a rapid pace.

The Importance of Continuous Integration (CI)

Continuous Integration (CI) is a cornerstone of modern software development practices, and its importance cannot be overstated. It transforms the way teams build and deliver software by promoting collaboration, quality assurance, and speed.

It is a game-changer in software development, offering these key advantages:

- **Early Issue Detection**: CI catches integration problems as soon as developers submit their code changes, making troubleshooting quicker and easier.
- **Consistency**: CI enforces uniformity in the development process, ensuring all code changes follow the same standards and practices.
- **Bugs Prevention**: Automated testing in CI identifies and prevents bugs early on, reducing the chances of defects reaching production.
- **Quick Feedback:** CI provides rapid feedback to developers, helping them fix issues promptly and boosting productivity.
- **Enhanced Collaboration**: CI encourages teamwork among developers, testers, and operations teams, promoting code quality and readiness.
- **Risk Reduction**: Small, incremental code changes in CI reduce the risk of complex and disruptive integrations.

- **Scalability**: CI scales efficiently, making it suitable for larger projects or growing teams.
- **Deployment Confidence**: CI ensures the reliability of code changes, instilling confidence in deployments, especially in Continuous Deployment (CD) environments.

CI revolutionizes software development by streamlining workflows, increasing code quality, and setting the stage for seamless Continuous Deployment.

Building an Effective CI Pipeline

A Continuous Integration (CI) pipeline is the backbone of automated software development. It streamlines the process of building, testing, and delivering code changes, ensuring that software remains consistently reliable. In this sub-chapter, we'll explore how to construct an effective CI pipeline and provide examples of common pipeline stages:

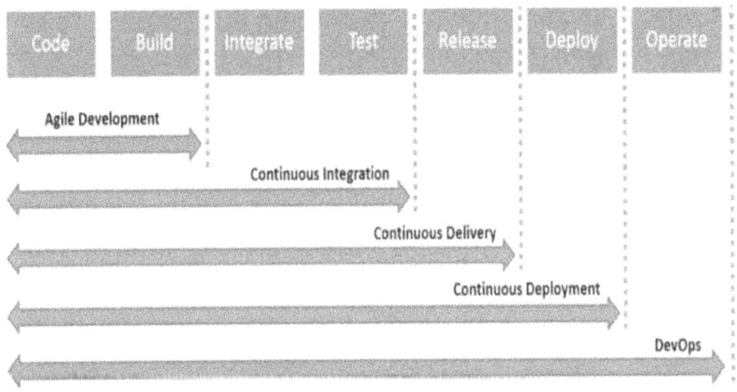

Components of a CI Pipeline:

- **Source Code Integration:** The CI pipeline starts with integrating code changes from multiple developers into a shared repository, often using version control systems like Git.

- **Automated Builds:** The pipeline automatically compiles the source code into executable artifacts. For example, in a Java project, this stage compiles Java source files into Java bytecode or JAR files.
- **Unit Testing**: Automated unit tests are executed to check individual code components for correctness. If any test fails, the pipeline halts, and developers are notified.
- **Code Quality Analysis**: Code quality tools, such as linters or static code analyzers, examine the codebase for adherence to coding standards and best practices.
- **Integration Testing**: After unit tests pass, the pipeline performs integration tests to ensure that different parts of the application work well together. This stage often involves deploying the application to a test environment.
- **Deployment to Staging**: In a CI/CD setup, the pipeline may deploy the application to a staging environment, closely resembling the production environment. This allows for thorough testing in a realistic setting.

- **User Acceptance Testing (UAT)**: In some cases, the pipeline deploys to a UAT environment for testing by stakeholders or end-users to validate new features or changes.
- **Security Scans:** Security scans, including vulnerability assessments and penetration tests, identify potential security issues within the application or its dependencies.
- **Performance Testing**: The pipeline may include performance testing to evaluate the application's behavior under various loads and conditions.
- **Artifact Packaging**: Once all tests pass, the pipeline packages the application into deployable artifacts, such as Docker images or distribution packages.
- **Deployment to Production**: In a CI/CD environment, this stage automatically deploys the application to production, often during off-peak hours to minimize user impact.
- **Monitoring Setup**: The pipeline can configure monitoring and alerting systems to ensure that the deployed application performs as expected.

Example CI Pipeline:

Here's a simplified example of a CI pipeline for a web application:

```
# .gitlab-ci.yml
stages:
  - build
  - test
  - deploy
variables:
  DOCKER_IMAGE_NAME: my-web-app
  DOCKER_REGISTRY: registry.example.com
  DOCKER_IMAGE_TAG: latest
  STAGING_ENV_URL: https://staging.my-web-
app.com
  PRODUCTION_ENV_URL:


before_script:
  - npm install  # Install project dependencies
build:
  stage: build
```

```
  script:
    - npm run build  # Build the web application
    - docker build -t
$DOCKER_IMAGE_NAME:$DOCKER_IMAGE_
TAG .  # Build Docker image
    - docker login -u $CI_REGISTRY_USER -p
$CI_REGISTRY_PASSWORD
$DOCKER_REGISTRY  # Log in to Docker
registry
    - docker push
$DOCKER_REGISTRY/$DOCKER_IMAGE_NA
ME:$DOCKER_IMAGE_TAG  # Push Docker
image to registry
  only:
    - master  # Run this stage only on the master
branch
test:
  stage: test
  script:
    - npm run test  # Run unit tests
    - npm run integration-test  # Run integration tests
  only:
```

```
    - master  # Run this stage only on the master
branch

deploy_staging:
  stage: deploy
  script:
    - docker pull
$DOCKER_REGISTRY/$DOCKER_IMAGE_NA
ME:$DOCKER_IMAGE_TAG  # Pull Docker
image from registry
    - docker-compose -f docker-compose.staging.yml
up -d  # Deploy to staging environment
  environment:
    name: staging
    url: $STAGING_ENV_URL
  only:
    - master  # Deploy to staging only on the master
branch
deploy_production:
  stage: deploy
  script:
    - docker pull
```

```
$DOCKER_REGISTRY/$DOCKER_IMAGE_NAME:$DOCKER_IMAGE_TAG  # Pull Docker image from registry
    - docker-compose -f docker-compose.production.yml up -d  # Deploy to production environment
  environment:
    name: production
    url: $PRODUCTION_ENV_URL
  only:
    - master  # Deploy to production only on the master branch
```

Explanation:

- his GitLab CI/CD pipeline consists of three stages: build, test, and deploy.

- In the build stage, it builds the Node.js application, creates a Docker image, and pushes it to a Docker registry.
- The test stage runs unit and integration tests to ensure code quality.
- The deploy stage deploys the application to a staging and production environment using Docker Compose. The staging environment is deployed on every push to the master branch, while production deployment can be manually triggered.
- The pipeline includes environment variables for configuration, such as Docker registry credentials and environment URLs.
- It only deploys to staging and production from the master branch, ensuring that deployments are controlled and predictable.

Please note that this is a simplified example. Depending on your project's complexity and requirements, you may need to customize and extend the pipeline to include additional steps such as security scans, database migrations, or notifications.

Automated Testing and Quality Assurance

In a CI environment, automated testing and quality

assurance play a pivotal role in ensuring that code changes are consistently validated for correctness, performance, and adherence to quality standards. Here, we'll explore how automated testing and quality assurance fit into the CI process:

- **Unit Tests**: Developers write tests for code changes. CI runs these tests automatically, catching issues early.
- **Integration Tests**: CI deploys the app to a test environment and tests how components work together.
- **End-to-End (E2E) Tests**: Automated E2E tests simulate user interactions and verify overall functionality.
- **Regression Tests**: CI prevents old issues from reappearing by running automated regression tests.
- **Quick Feedback**: CI provides rapid feedback to developers, enabling prompt issue resolution.
- **Code Quality Analysis**: CI checks code quality and enforces coding standards.
- **Performance and Security Tests**: CI can

include automated performance and security tests, identifying issues early.

In summary, automated testing and quality assurance are integral parts of the CI process. They provide a safety net that allows code changes to be integrated and deployed with confidence. By automating these tests, CI ensures that code quality remains consistent, defects are caught early, and the development process is efficient and reliable.

Test Automation Tools:

- **Unit Testing Frameworks:** For unit tests, popular frameworks include JUnit (Java), pytest (Python), and Jest (JavaScript).
- **Integration and E2E Testing Tools:** Tools like Selenium, Cypress, and Puppeteer are commonly used for integration and E2E tests.

- **Test Runners**: Test runners like JUnit Runner, TestNG, or Mocha (for JavaScript) execute tests and provide test results.

- **Continuous Integration Tools:** CI/CD platforms such as Jenkins, Travis CI, GitLab CI/CD, and CircleCI automate the execution of tests in pipelines.

Sample Test Automation Workflow:

Let's take a simplified example of a test automation workflow for a web application:

- **Unit Tests**: Developers write unit tests for individual functions or modules to ensure they work correctly.
- **Integration Tests**: Integration tests validate that different parts of the application (e.g., frontend and backend) work together as expected.
- **E2E Tests**: E2E tests simulate user interactions with the web application. For instance, they can click buttons, fill out forms, and verify that the application responds correctly.

- **Test Automation Framework:** A testing

framework (e.g., Jasmine for JavaScript) is used to organize and run tests. CI/CD tools are configured to execute these tests automatically.

- **Continuous Integration**: Whenever code changes are pushed to the version control system (e.g., Git), the CI/CD pipeline is triggered. This pipeline builds the application, deploys it to a testing environment, and runs automated tests.
- **Reporting**: Test results are generated and reported, indicating which tests passed and which failed. Developers receive immediate feedback.
- **Continuous Deployment**: If all tests pass successfully, the code can proceed to deployment in a staging or production environment.

Sample Test Case 1: Unit Test

Test Case Name: **testAdditionFunction**

Description: This unit test verifies the correctness of the addition function in a calculator application.

Test Steps:

1. Input two numbers, e.g., 5 and 3.
2. Call the addition function with these input numbers.
3. Verify that the result is 8, which is the expected sum.

Expected Result: The addition function should return 8 when given inputs 5 and 3.

Sample Test Case 2: End-to-End (E2E) Test

Test Case Name: **testUserLogin**

Description: This E2E test verifies the user login functionality of a web application.

Test Steps:

1. Open the web application's login page.
2. Enter valid login credentials (e.g., username: "testuser," password: "password123").

3. Click the "Login" button.
4. Verify that the application navigates to the user's dashboard or home page.

Expected Result: After successful login, the application should display the user's dashboard or home page.

Integrating Static Code Analysis into CI/CD Pipelines

Static code analysis is a critical practice that helps ensure code quality, identify potential issues, and maintain coding standards. In a CI/CD pipeline, integrating static code analysis tools is essential for catching code problems early in the development process. Here's how it works:

- **Code Analysis Tools**: Choose a static code analysis tool or a combination of tools that fit your project's programming languages and requirements. Popular tools include ESLint for JavaScript, Pylint for Python, and SonarQube, which supports multiple languages.
- **Configuration**: Configure the selected code analysis tool to define coding standards, best practices, and rules that your code should follow. Customize the tool to align with your project's specific coding guidelines and requirements.
- **Automated Execution**: Within your CI/CD pipeline, set up a dedicated stage or job for static code analysis. This stage is triggered

automatically whenever code changes are pushed to the repository.

- **Code Scanning:** The static code analysis tool scans the codebase, examining every file and line of code for adherence to the defined rules. It identifies issues such as code smells, potential bugs, security vulnerabilities, and style violations.
- **Results Reporting**: After the analysis is complete, the tool generates a report that highlights issues found within the code. The report includes details about each problem, its location in the code, and suggestions for resolution.
- **Quality Gate**: Some static code analysis tools support the concept of quality gates. These gates define a set of criteria that code changes must meet to be considered acceptable. If the code changes don't meet the quality gate's criteria, the CI/CD pipeline can fail, preventing the integration of problematic code.
- **Feedback to Developers**: In the CI/CD pipeline, the results of the static code analysis are

communicated to developers. This feedback loop is crucial, as it allows developers to review and address issues promptly.

- **Continuous Improvement**: Code analysis tools often provide historical data and trends, allowing teams to track code quality over time. Teams can use this information to identify areas for improvement and refine their coding standards.

Benefits:

- **Early Issue Detection**: Static code analysis catches issues at the earliest stages of development, reducing the likelihood of defects reaching production.
- **Consistency**: It enforces coding standards and best practices, ensuring a consistent codebase even as the project scales.
- **Security**: Static code analysis can identify security vulnerabilities, helping to mitigate risks.
- **Maintainability**: Cleaner code is easier to maintain, reducing technical debt.
- **Efficiency**: Automated analysis is faster and

more consistent than manual code reviews.

Example: In a CI/CD pipeline, you might use ESLint for a JavaScript project. When developers push code changes, the pipeline runs ESLint to identify issues such as unused variables, incorrect indentation, or security concerns. If any issues are found, the pipeline can fail, preventing the integration of problematic code. Developers receive feedback and can make corrections before code changes progress further in the pipeline.

Some of the popular tools used:

- ESLint (JavaScript)
- Pylint (Python)
- SonarQube
- Checkmarx(Security)
- TSLint (TypeScript)

Strategies for Continuous Deployment

Continuous Deployment (CD) is an advanced DevOps practice that involves automatically deploying code changes to production environments after passing through a series of automated tests and validations.To successfully implement continuous deployment, consider the following strategies:

1. **Establish a Strong Continuous Integration (CI) Foundation:**

   Continuous deployment builds upon a solid CI foundation. In CI, developers regularly merge code changes into a shared repository. Automated tests, including unit tests, integration tests, and code analysis, validate these changes. This practice ensures that code is tested comprehensively before it enters the CD pipeline.

2. **Implement Comprehensive Automated Testing:**
   Automated testing is a cornerstone of CD. Develop a suite of tests that cover different aspects of your application. This includes unit tests to verify individual components, integration tests to check how various parts interact, end-to-end (E2E) tests for user workflows, performance tests, and security tests. For example, in a web application, you might use tools like Selenium for E2E testing and OWASP ZAP for security scanning.

3. **Feature Toggles (Feature Flags):**
   Feature toggles or feature flags allow you to control the release of new features independently of the code deployment. For instance, you can deploy a feature but keep it hidden from users until it's thoroughly tested and ready for release. Feature flags give you flexibility and the ability to roll back a feature quickly if issues arise.

4. **Build Separate Deployment Pipelines:**

Create separate deployment pipelines for different environments, such as staging and production. Staging environments should closely mimic production to catch any environment-specific issues early. This separation ensures that code moves through controlled stages before reaching production.

5. **Implement Automated Deployment Scripts:** Develop automated deployment scripts or use deployment automation tools like Ansible, Puppet, or Kubernetes. These scripts ensure consistency in the deployment process. Infrastructure as Code (IaC) principles can also be applied to manage and provision infrastructure

6. **Use Rolling Deployments:** Rolling deployments minimize downtime and user impact. In a blue-green deployment, you maintain two identical environments: one with the current version (blue) and one with the new version (green). You gradually shift traffic from the blue to the green environment. If issues arise, you can quickly switch back to the stable blue

environment.

7. **Prioritize Monitoring and Observability:** Robust monitoring and observability are crucial in CD. Tools like Prometheus, Grafana, and ELK Stack help you gain real-time insights into your application's performance and health. Monitor application logs, metrics, and user behavior to detect and respond to issues promptly.
8. **Automated Rollback Procedures:** Automated rollback procedures should be in place in case issues are detected after deployment. If your monitoring systems trigger alarms or metrics indicating problems, automated rollback scripts should revert to the previous stable version. For instance, if a new version of a web application starts returning error rates above a certain threshold, the CD pipeline can automatically trigger a rollback to the previous version.

9. **Version Control and Artifact Management:** Use version control systems like Git to track

code changes and manage different versions of your application. Additionally, maintain an artifact management system (e.g., Nexus or JFrog Artifactory) to store and organize binary artifacts, ensuring traceability and easy rollback to previous versions if necessary.

10. **Security and Compliance Checks:**

    Integrate automated security scans and compliance checks into your CD pipeline. Tools like Checkmarx or SonarQube can identify security vulnerabilities and compliance violations. Ensuring that security and compliance are validated as part of the deployment process is essential, especially for regulated industries.

11. **Documentation and Runbooks:**

    Maintain clear and up-to-date documentation and runbooks for the deployment process. This documentation should include step-by-step instructions for deployment, rollback procedures, and troubleshooting guides. Examples of runbook procedures may include how to monitor application logs or how to restore a database backup during a rollback.

12. **Foster Collaboration and Communication:** Collaboration between development, operations, and security teams is critical for successful CD. Establish communication channels and practices that allow teams to collaborate effectively. For example, regular cross-team meetings or the use of collaboration tools like Slack can facilitate communication.

13. **Continuous Improvement:** Continuously gather feedback from deployments and monitoring systems. Use this feedback to improve the deployment process, automation scripts, and overall system reliability. Metrics such as Mean Time to Recovery (MTTR) can help measure the effectiveness of your CD practices.

14. **User Feedback and A/B Testing:**

    Collect user feedback through channels like customer support or feedback forms. Additionally, conduct A/B testing to evaluate the impact of new features or changes on user experience. Analyzing user feedback and A/B test results helps make informed decisions about feature releases and improvements.

Continuous deployment is a powerful DevOps practice that enables teams to deliver code changes to users rapidly and reliably. By following these strategies and integrating them into your CD pipeline, you can ensure that your application maintains a high level of quality and stability even as you accelerate the pace of development and deployment.

CHAPTER 8

Microservices Architecture

Understanding Microservices and their Benefits

Microservices architecture is a way of designing and building software applications as a collection of small, independent services that work together to provide a complete application. Each of these services is like a tiny application on its own, focused on performing a specific task or function. Let's break down the concept and explore its benefits:

1. **Small and Focused Services:**

Microservices are small and focused on a particular job. For example, in an e-commerce application, you might have a microservice for handling product catalog, another for processing orders, and yet another for managing customer accounts. Each microservice has its own dedicated task.

2. **Independent and Scalable:**

   Microservices can be developed, deployed, and scaled independently. This means that if one part of your application needs more resources or updates, you can work on just that microservice without affecting the rest of the application. It's like changing a single piece of a puzzle without redoing the entire picture.

3. **Technology Diversity:**

   Microservices allow you to use different technologies for different parts of your application. For instance, you might use one programming language or database for one microservice and a completely different set of technologies for another. This flexibility lets you choose the right tools for each job.

4. **Fault Isolation:**

   If one microservice encounters a problem or crashes, it doesn't bring down the entire application. Only the affected microservice is affected, while the rest continue to work. This makes your application more resilient and fault-tolerant.

5. **Continuous Deployment:**

   Because microservices are independent, you can update and deploy them frequently without disrupting the entire application. This allows you to release new features and fixes more rapidly, keeping your application up to date and responsive to user needs.

6. **Improved Team Collaboration:**

   Microservices architecture often leads to smaller,

focused teams that can work more independently on their respective microservices. This can enhance collaboration and streamline development efforts.

7. **Scalability:**
   You can scale individual microservices as needed. For example, if your e-commerce application experiences high traffic during holidays, you can scale up the order processing microservice to handle the load without affecting other parts of the application.

8. **Easier Maintenance and Testing:**
   Smaller codebases are easier to maintain and test. When you have a problem or need to add a new feature, you can do so in a specific microservice without worrying about unintended consequences elsewhere.

In summary, microservices architecture breaks down complex applications into smaller, manageable pieces, offering benefits like independence, scalability, flexibility, and easier maintenance. It's like building with LEGO blocks, where each block (microservice) has a specific function but can be combined to create something much larger and more powerful. However, it's essential to plan and design your microservices carefully to fully reap these benefits.

Designing and Implementing Microservices

Designing and implementing microservices is a critical step in adopting a microservices architecture. Below, we'll discuss the key considerations and provide examples to illustrate the process.

1. **Define Microservice Boundaries:**
   Start by identifying the boundaries of your microservices. Each microservice should have a clear and specific responsibility. For example, in an e-commerce application, you could have microservices for product catalog, order processing, user authentication, and payment processing.

2. **Choose the Right Technologies:**
   Select technologies that align with the specific needs of each microservice. For instance, if you're building a product catalog microservice, you might choose a NoSQL database like MongoDB for flexible data storage.
3. **Communication and APIs:**
   Decide how your microservices will communicate with each other. Most microservices communicate through HTTP-based APIs (RESTful or GraphQL). Define clear API contracts for communication between microservices. For example, the product catalog

microservice might expose APIs to retrieve product details or update inventory.

4. **Data Management:**

   Consider how data will be managed. Microservices can have their own databases (private data storage) or share databases (shared data storage). For instance, the order processing microservice may use a shared database to store order data.

5. **Stateless vs. Stateful Microservices:**

   Determine whether your microservices will be stateless or stateful. Stateless microservices are independent and don't store user-specific data, making them easier to scale. Stateful microservices may maintain user sessions or specific application states. Choose the appropriate approach based on your application's requirements.

6. **Scalability:**

   Design your microservices for scalability. For example, if you anticipate high traffic for the user authentication microservice, you should architect it to handle load balancing and scaling.

7. **Error Handling and Resilience:**
   Implement robust error handling and resilience mechanisms. Microservices should gracefully handle failures, retries, and timeouts. For instance, when calling a payment processing microservice, consider how it handles payment failures and retries.

8. **Security:**
   Implement security measures to protect your microservices. Authenticate and authorize API requests between microservices. Apply security best practices to safeguard data and prevent unauthorized access.

9. **Monitoring and Logging:**
   Implement monitoring and logging for each

microservice. Tools like Prometheus and Grafana can help you monitor performance and troubleshoot issues. For example, you might set up logging in the order processing microservice to track order status changes.

10. **Testing: -**
 Conduct extensive testing, including unit tests, integration tests, and end-to-end tests for each microservice. For example, when building the user authentication microservice, you'd write tests to ensure that user login and registration work correctly.

11. **Deployment and Containerization: -**
 Containerize your microservices using technologies like Docker. This simplifies deployment and ensures consistent environments. Use container orchestration platforms like Kubernetes to manage microservice deployments and scaling. For instance, you can use Kubernetes to deploy and manage multiple instances of the payment processing microservice.

12. **Continuous Integration and Deployment**

(CI/CD): -

Implement CI/CD pipelines for each microservice to automate testing and deployment. CI/CD tools like Jenkins or GitLab CI can help streamline the process. For example, you can set up CI/CD for the product catalog microservice to automatically deploy code changes to a staging environment for testing.

13. **Documentation: -**

Document each microservice's API, including endpoints, request/response formats, and authentication requirements. Clear documentation helps developers understand how to interact with your microservices. For instance, you'd document the API endpoints and expected payload for the order processing microservice.

14. **Versioning**: -

Establish versioning practices for your microservices. When making changes to APIs, use version numbers to ensure backward compatibility. For example, the user authentication microservice's API might include versioning in the URL (e.g.,

/v1/auth/login).

15. **Monitoring in Production:** -

    Implement production monitoring to track the health and performance of your microservices. Tools like New Relic or Datadog can help you detect issues and optimize performance. For instance, you can set up alerts to notify you if the payment processing microservice experiences high latency.

    Example:

    - Let's consider an example of a ride-sharing application. You could have microservices for user management, ride booking, payment processing, and driver location tracking. Each microservice has specific responsibilities and APIs for interactions. The user management microservice handles user registration and authentication, while the ride booking microservice manages ride requests and matches riders with drivers.

      By carefully designing and implementing your microservices, you can create a flexible and scalable architecture that supports rapid development and deployment while ensuring reliability and maintainability.

Service Discovery and Communication Patterns

Service discovery and communication patterns are essential components of a microservices architecture that enable different microservices to find and communicate with each other efficiently. Let's explore these concepts briefly:

Service Discovery:

- **What It Is:** Service discovery is a mechanism that allows microservices to dynamically discover and locate other microservices within a distributed system.
- **How It Works**: When a microservice needs to communicate with another, it queries a service registry or discovery server. The service registry maintains a list of available services and their network locations (e.g., IP addresses and ports).

- **Example**: In a ride-sharing application, the ride booking microservice may need to find the driver location microservice to determine the nearest available driver. It queries the service registry to discover the driver location microservice's network location.

Communication Patterns:

- **Request-Response**: In this pattern, one microservice sends a request to another and waits for a response. It's similar to a client-server interaction.
- **Publish-Subscribe**: Microservices can publish events or messages to a topic or channel, and other microservices can subscribe to these events. This pattern is often used for asynchronous communication and event-driven architectures.
- **Remote Procedure Call (RPC)**: Microservices can invoke remote methods or procedures provided by other microservices. It's like one

microservice asking another to perform a specific action on its behalf.

- **Message Queues:** Message queues facilitate communication by allowing microservices to send messages to queues, and other microservices can consume messages from those queues. This pattern ensures decoupling and reliability.

Why They Matter:

- **Scalability**: Service discovery enables automatic scaling of microservices, as new instances can be discovered and added to the system easily.
- **Resilience**: Communication patterns help microservices maintain resilience by providing alternatives when one microservice fails.
- **Flexibility**: Microservices can use different communication patterns based on specific use cases. For example, request-response for synchronous interactions and message queues for asynchronous processing.

- **Decoupling**: These patterns reduce tight coupling between microservices, making the architecture more flexible and easier to maintain.

In summary, service discovery allows microservices to find each other, while communication patterns dictate how they interact. These components are crucial for building robust and scalable microservices-based systems.

Managing Data in a Microservices Environment

Managing data in a microservices environment presents unique challenges and opportunities. Microservices architecture encourages the decomposition of applications into smaller, focused services, each with its data store. Here's a brief overview of how data management works in a microservices setup:

1. **Microservices Data Stores:**
   In a microservices architecture, each microservice often has its own data store. This allows microservices to be independent and have control over their specific data requirements. For example, a user management microservice might use a relational database to store user profiles, while a product catalog microservice might use a

NoSQL database to manage product information.

2. **Data Ownership:**

   Each microservice is responsible for the data it owns. This includes creating, updating, deleting, and retrieving data within its data store. Microservices should not directly access the data stores of other services to maintain separation and independence.

3. **Data Consistency:**

   Ensuring data consistency across microservices can be challenging. Distributed transactions are often avoided in microservices due to their complexity and potential performance impact. Instead, microservices often rely on eventual consistency, where data consistency is guaranteed over time but not necessarily immediately.

4. **Communication via APIs:**

Microservices communicate with each other through well-defined APIs. Data is exchanged via API calls, typically using HTTP or messaging protocols. For instance, a shopping cart microservice might call the product catalog microservice's API to retrieve product details.

5. **Event-Driven Data Flow:**

   Event-driven architectures are common in microservices. Microservices emit events when they make changes to their data. Other microservices can subscribe to these events to update their own data or take necessary actions. This decouples services and supports real-time data updates.

6. **Data Synchronization:**

   Some microservices may need to replicate or synchronize data from other services. For instance, a reporting microservice might periodically synchronize data from various source microservices to generate reports.

7. **API Gateway:**

An API gateway can be used to provide a unified entry point for client applications. It can aggregate data from multiple microservices and present it as a single API, simplifying client interactions.

8. **Caching:**

   Caching mechanisms can help improve performance by reducing the need to make repeated requests to data stores. Caches can be placed at various layers, such as within microservices or at the API gateway.

9. **Data Backups and Recovery:**

   Each microservice should have a strategy for data backups and recovery. This ensures that critical data is not lost in case of failures or data corruption.

10. **Data Security and Access Control:** -

    Microservices must implement robust security

measures to protect their data stores. Access control, encryption, and authentication mechanisms should be in place to prevent unauthorized access.

11. **Database Technologies: -**
    The choice of database technologies should align with the specific requirements of each microservice. Relational databases, NoSQL databases, key-value stores, and column-family databases can all be used as appropriate.
12. **Data Migration and Versioning: -**
    As microservices evolve, data schemas may change. Data migration and versioning strategies are crucial to ensure that existing data remains compatible with newer versions of microservices.

Managing data in a microservices environment requires careful planning and adherence to best practices. While microservices offer benefits such as scalability and independence, they also introduce complexities in data management that must be addressed to build a successful microservices-based application.

Embedding Security Practices in Microservices

Embedding security practices in microservices is crucial to protect your application and its data. Here's a brief summary of key security considerations:

1. **Authentication and Authorization:** Implement strong authentication and authorization mechanisms for microservices to ensure that only authorized users or services can access data and

functionalities.

2. **Secure API Design:** Design APIs with security in mind, using standards like OAuth 2.0 and JWT (JSON Web Tokens) for secure authentication and authorization.
3. **Input Validation:** Sanitize and validate input data to prevent common security vulnerabilities like SQL injection and cross-site scripting (XSS).
4. **Data Encryption:** Encrypt sensitive data both in transit and at rest. Use HTTPS for communication and secure storage mechanisms for data.
5. **Security Testing**: Regularly conduct security testing, including vulnerability assessments, penetration testing, and code reviews, to identify and remediate vulnerabilities.
6. **Patch Management**: Keep all software components, including libraries and dependencies, up to date with the latest security patches to prevent known vulnerabilities.
7. **Least Privilege Principle:** Follow the principle of least privilege, ensuring that microservices have

only the permissions necessary to perform their tasks.

8. **Monitoring and Logging:** Implement robust monitoring and logging to detect and respond to security incidents promptly. Use tools like intrusion detection systems and security information and event management (SIEM) solutions.
9. **Threat Modeling:** Conduct threat modeling exercises to identify potential security threats and vulnerabilities early in the development process.
10. **Access Control Lists (ACLs):** - Use access control lists to restrict access to sensitive resources or APIs based on user roles and permissions.

ii.

1. **Container Security:** - If using containerization, ensure container security by regularly scanning container images for vulnerabilities and following best practices for secure container deployment.
2. **Secrets Management:** - Safeguard sensitive information such as API keys, passwords, and

certificates using secure secrets management tools.

3. **Compliance and Regulatory Requirements: -** Ensure that your microservices comply with industry-specific regulations and standards, such as GDPR, HIPAA, or PCI DSS, if applicable.
4. **Incident Response Plan: -** Develop an incident response plan that outlines the steps to take in case of a security breach. Test this plan periodically to ensure readiness.
5. **Security Culture: -** Foster a security-aware culture within your development and operations teams. Educate team members about security best practices and the importance of security in the microservices environment.

Embedding security practices in microservices is an ongoing process that requires continuous vigilance and adaptation to emerging threats. By proactively addressing security concerns, you can build a resilient and trustworthy microservices-based application.

Best Practices for MicroServices Design

Designing microservices effectively is critical for building a scalable, maintainable, and resilient application. Here are some best practices to consider when designing microservices:

1. **Single Responsibility Principle (SRP):** Each microservice should have a single, well-defined responsibility or purpose. Avoid creating monolithic services that handle multiple unrelated tasks.
2. **Decoupling:** Aim for loose coupling between microservices. Minimize direct dependencies and use well-defined APIs for communication. Decoupling allows for independent development, scaling, and maintenance.
3. **Independent Data Stores**: Microservices should have their own data stores (private data). Avoid sharing databases between microservices to prevent tight coupling and data consistency issues.
4. **Service Contracts:** Clearly define and document API contracts for microservices, including request/response formats and error handling. Maintain backward compatibility when making

changes to APIs.

5. **Stateless Services:** Strive for stateless microservices whenever possible. Maintain state externally or use caching solutions to ensure scalability and fault tolerance.
6. **Distributed Systems Thinking:** Treat your microservices architecture as a distributed system. Account for network latency, failures, and partial outages when designing interactions between services.
7. **API Gateway:** Consider using an API gateway to provide a unified entry point for client applications. It can aggregate data from multiple microservices, reducing client complexity.
8. **Event-Driven Architecture:** Embrace event-driven patterns for asynchronous communication between microservices. Events allow for real-time updates and decoupled interactions.

9. **Circuit Breaker Pattern:** Implement the circuit breaker pattern to handle failures gracefully and prevent cascading failures in case of service unavailability.

10. **Monitoring and Logging: -** Implement robust monitoring and logging for each microservice. Use tools like Prometheus, Grafana, and ELK Stack to gain insights into performance and troubleshoot issues.
11. **Containerization and Orchestration: -** Containerize microservices using technologies like Docker and manage them with container orchestration platforms like Kubernetes. This simplifies deployment and scaling.
12. **Continuous Integration and Deployment (CI/CD): -** Establish CI/CD pipelines for each microservice to automate testing and deployment. This accelerates the development and release process.
13. **Load Balancing: -** Employ load balancing to distribute traffic evenly across multiple instances of a microservice, ensuring high availability and scalability.

14. **Security by Design: -** Embed security practices into microservices from the beginning. Implement authentication, authorization, encryption, and

secure API design.

15. **Versioning:** - Use versioning for APIs to ensure backward compatibility when introducing changes. Include version information in the API endpoints.
16. **Error Handling:** - Implement consistent error-handling strategies and return informative error messages to clients for easier troubleshooting.
17. **Documentation:** - Maintain thorough documentation for each microservice, including API documentation, deployment procedures, and architecture diagrams.
18. **Scalability:** - Design microservices with scalability in mind. Horizontal scaling (adding more instances) should be straightforward to accommodate increased load.
19. **Testing Strategies:** - Implement comprehensive testing, including unit tests, integration tests, and end-to-end tests. Test microservices in isolation and as part of the entire system.

20. **Compliance and Governance:** - Ensure that microservices adhere to regulatory and

compliance requirements relevant to your industry (e.g., GDPR, HIPAA).

These best practices are foundational for creating a well-structured microservices architecture that can adapt to evolving business needs and deliver a reliable and responsive application. Tailor these practices to suit your specific project and continuously iterate on your microservices design as your application evolves.

CHAPTER 9

Monitoring and Observability

Introduction to Monitoring and Observability

Monitoring and observability are essential pillars of modern DevOps practices, providing insights and actionable data to ensure the reliability, performance, and availability of complex software systems. In today's dynamic and distributed environments, where applications span multiple services, micro-services, containers, and cloud platforms, monitoring and observability have become integral to maintaining operational excellence.

Monitoring involves the systematic collection, measurement, and analysis of various metrics and indicators that reflect the health and performance of an application or infrastructure. Monitoring tools enable DevOps teams to track metrics like CPU usage, memory consumption, response times, and error rates. These metrics help identify bottlenecks, anomalies, and trends that can impact user experience and system reliability. Monitoring also facilitates capacity planning and resource optimization, allowing teams to scale resources up or down as needed.

Observability, on the other hand, goes beyond traditional monitoring by providing contextual insights into the internal workings of applications and systems. It focuses on understanding how components interact, tracing requests as they traverse through various services, and diagnosing the root causes of issues. Observability tools empower DevOps teams to collect and correlate logs, traces, and metrics, creating a holistic view of system behavior. This enables quicker detection, diagnosis, and resolution of incidents, enhancing the Mean Time to Resolution (MTTR) and minimizing downtime.

To achieve effective monitoring and observability, DevOps teams leverage a range of tools and practices. They instrument code with logging and tracing statements, ensuring that critical events and transactions are captured. They also deploy metrics collectors to gather data from different layers of the application stack. Centralized logging platforms aggregate logs from various sources, providing a unified view for analysis and troubleshooting. Distributed tracing tools map requests across services, revealing bottlenecks and latency issues. Dashboards and visualization tools present real-time and historical data, aiding in trend analysis and decision-making.

In the context of a DevOps book, delving into monitoring and observability is crucial. This includes explaining the differences between the two concepts, discussing the selection and configuration of monitoring tools, demonstrating the creation of meaningful dashboards, and showcasing how observability practices improve incident response and contribute to a culture of continuous improvement. By integrating these practices, DevOps practitioners can proactively identify issues, enhance system performance, and deliver exceptional user experiences in today's complex and dynamic technological landscape.

Choosing the Right Monitoring Tools and Metrics

As IT infrastructures become increasingly distributed and complex, cybersecurity administrators struggle to protect users, data, applications, systems and networks from attacks. Layers upon layers of virtualization, containerization and fabric overlays make it difficult for security teams to properly view their network, identify threats and remediate them in a reasonable amount of time.

Advanced security tools that incorporate AI and machine learning capabilities tout their ability to provide security clarity in first- and third-party infrastructures, as well as the various software-defined-network layers. At the same time, confusion has mounted over the roles of security observability vs. visibility and monitoring. Some see the three terms as interchangeable, but there are distinct differences that can affect how these security tools and processes interact

Process of monitoring and alerting

A tool in a larger monitoring toolset is typically configured by an IT security administrator to ingest various device or software logs, simple network management protocol polls and traps, event messages, netflow, packet capture and other streaming telemetry data. Triggers are usually set up, so when a security monitoring tool processes an event that matches a specific circumstance or meets a certain threshold, an alert is issued. This alert is fielded by IT security staff to identify whether it is a valid security threat, determine the root cause of the security incident and remediate the threat. But traditional security monitoring tools take a large amount of administrator time to hunt down and resolve an incident using manual processes. The problem is magnified as infrastructures become more complex and more monitoring data is collected. Additionally, security incidents often generate alerts sourced from multiple security monitoring tools.

Monitoring tools

Tools generally are chosen based on a variety of factors like usability, cost, skill of the resources configuring and using it. A few tools that are used in enterprises are highlighted below:

1. **Nagios** is a popular and powerful tool that can monitor servers as well as applications in Windows / Linux environments. Nagios also excels in its flexibility and extensibility. Its modular design allows users to create custom plugins tailored to their specific monitoring requirements. Moreover, Nagios provides a web-based interface that offers a centralized view of monitored systems and their status, making it easier for administrators to manage and

troubleshoot issues. Additionally, Nagios can be integrated with other IT management tools, such as ticketing systems and reporting tools, for a more comprehensive monitoring and response strategy. Overall, Nagios is an indispensable tool for IT teams, enabling them to proactively monitor their infrastructure, reduce downtime, and ensure the efficient operation of critical services in today's complex and dynamic IT environments.

2. **https://prometheus.lo** Prometheus is a leading open-source monitoring and alerting system designed for the dynamic and cloud-native infrastructure prevalent in modern IT environments. It excels in its ability to gather metrics and monitor the health and performance of applications and services in real-time. Prometheus follows a pull-based model where it scrapes metrics from instrumented targets (e.g., application instances, servers, or containers) at regular intervals. This approach offers great flexibility as it supports a wide range of data sources, making it suitable for monitoring

everything from microservices and cloud resources to traditional server-based applications. Prometheus also provides a powerful query language called PromQL, which enables users to express complex queries and create custom alerts based on collected metrics. With its extensive ecosystem of exporters and integrations, Prometheus has become a cornerstone in the DevOps and cloud-native monitoring landscape, allowing organizations to gain deep insights into their systems' behavior and troubleshoot issues effectively. One of Prometheus' standout features is its robust alerting and notification system. Users can define alerting rules in Prometheus based on specific conditions and thresholds within the collected metrics. When an alert rule is triggered, Prometheus can send notifications through various communication channels, such as email, Slack, or third-party incident management systems. This proactive alerting mechanism helps organizations quickly identify and respond to anomalies or performance degradations in their infrastructure, ultimately reducing downtime and improving service reliability. Furthermore, Prometheus integrates seamlessly with Grafana, a popular visualization and dash-boarding tool, enabling users to create dynamic and informative dashboards to visualize their monitoring data effectively. Overall, Prometheus has become an essential tool for monitoring and maintaining the health and performance of modern, distributed systems, and it continues to evolve to meet the demands of today's rapidly changing IT landscape.

3. **www.newrelic.com** New Relic is a robust application performance monitoring (APM) tool that provides deep insights into the performance and health of applications and infrastructure in modern digital environments. It offers comprehensive observability across the entire technology stack, from end-user experiences and application code to underlying infrastructure components. New Relic's strength lies in its ability to collect and analyze data from diverse sources, including web and mobile applications,

microservices, servers, containers, and more. This data is presented in a unified dashboard, allowing organizations to gain a holistic view of their environment. New Relic's APM capabilities enable users to pinpoint performance bottlenecks, trace transactions, and identify the root causes of issues, ultimately improving application reliability and end-user satisfaction. In addition to APM, New Relic offers features like infrastructure monitoring, synthetic monitoring, and error tracking. The platform also includes AI-driven anomaly detection and alerting, which can proactively identify abnormal behavior and notify teams before issues impact users. Moreover, New Relic Insights provides a powerful querying and visualization engine, enabling users to create custom dashboards and gain deeper insights into their data. It includes support for popular cloud platforms like AWS and Azure.

4. **www.datadog.com** DataDog is an exceptional monitoring and analytics platform that is proven

to be an invaluable asset for many organizations. With its comprehensive suite of monitoring and observability tools, DataDog empowers users to gain deep insights into the performance, availability, and health of our complex IT infrastructure. One of DataDog's standout features is its ability to provide real-time visibility across our entire technology stack. By effortlessly integrating with a wide array of technologies and platforms, including cloud services, containers, databases, and more, DataDog aggregates and correlates data from various sources into a unified dashboard. This consolidated view allows us to identify issues quickly, troubleshoot efficiently, and make informed decisions to optimize any systems' performance. DataDog's robust alerting and notification capabilities significantly improve incident response times. With customizable alerting thresholds and intelligent anomaly detection, potential problems can be proactively detected and addressed before they impact the end-users. The platform possesses flexibility in alerting mechanisms, such as email, SMS, and integrations with collaboration tools like Slack, ensures that the right team members are promptly notified when issues arise, facilitating swift resolution. DataDog's data visualization and reporting features have transformed the way analysis and critical insights are propagated across the organization.

5. **www.splunk.com** is a well known tool used industry wide for data assimilation/ingestion, building in-sights from the ingested data and alerting on events of interest based on set parameters that are of interest.

Implementing the Real-Time Monitoring and Alerting

Implementing real-time monitoring and alerting is like having a vigilant guardian for your application, keeping a watchful eye on its health 24/7. Key performance metrics such as response time, error rates, **CPU utilization, memory usage, and network latency** act as the **vital signs** of your application's well-being. Imagine you're running an e-commerce platform, and response time is a critical metric. You set a threshold that triggers an alert if response times exceed 500 milliseconds for three consecutive data points. This means that if your application's responsiveness suddenly deteriorates, you'll receive an immediate alert, prompting your team to investigate and take corrective action before customers start experiencing slowdowns.

Furthermore, anomaly detection algorithms are the silent sentinels, capable of **spotting unusual patterns** in your metrics. For instance, a sudden spike in error rates or a drop in memory usage may indicate an emerging issue. **Anomaly detection** can raise alerts, even before traditional threshold-based rules trigger, allowing for swift intervention. **Prioritizing alerts** is crucial; critical alerts require immediate attention, while lower-priority ones can be handled during routine maintenance. An incident response playbook guides your team on how to react systematically, ensuring efficient resolution. Real-time dashboards provide at-a-glance visibility, showcasing the current state of your application. For instance, you can create a dashboard displaying response time, error rates, and resource utilization, allowing you to monitor user experience and system performance in real-time. By continuously improving alerting rules and procedures, training your team, and reviewing alerts for relevance, you'll maintain a robust real-time monitoring and alerting system that ensures the health and reliability of your application.

Some of the key points to note here are:

- Watchful Guardian
- Vital Signs
- Immediate Alerts
- Spotting Odd Behavior
- Priority Alerts
- Action Plan
- Dashboard
- Continuous Improvement

In simple terms, real-time monitoring and alerting help keep your application healthy and fast. They watch for problems and tell us when something's not right, so we can fix it quickly. It's like having a superhero for your app!

Application Performance Monitoring and Log Management

Application performance monitoring is a critical aspect of ensuring the smooth operation of production applications. It involves various methodologies and considerations that can be tailored to your organization's specific needs. Let's delve deeper into some of these aspects:

1. **Application Criticality:** The criticality of an application determines the depth and extent of performance monitoring required. High-traffic web applications, for example, demand comprehensive monitoring to maintain optimal functionality and prevent business disruptions. Consider the following monitoring strategies:
    - Web Applications: Monitor ports for availability, check infrastructure for abnormalities, and analyze application logs for critical errors.
    - Stand-alone or Cloud Applications: Focus on monitoring both infrastructure and application logs.
2. **Technology Stack:** The technology stack used in your application influences your monitoring tools

and strategies. Different technologies may require specialized **monitoring** solutions. For instance, a Java-based application may benefit from Java-specific monitoring tools.

3. **Infrastructure Considerations:** Depending on whether your application is hosted on-premises or in the cloud, your **monitoring** tools and capabilities may vary. On-premises infrastructure limits your choices to what can be installed and integrated with the existing environment, while cloud environments offer a broader range of monitoring options.

4. **Compliance and Governance Requirements:** Adherence to **compliance** and governance standards is essential, especially for applications handling sensitive data or serving specific industries. The choice and level of compliance are often dictated by the application's use case:
   - Defense Applications: Must adhere to strict compliance standards like NIST 800-53rev5.

   - Healthcare Applications: Governed by

HIPAA regulations.

- Cybersecurity Applications: May align with frameworks such as the Mitre framework.

5. **Real-Time Monitoring:** Real-time monitoring tools provide instant insights into the performance of your **application**. They can detect anomalies, bottlenecks, and errors as they occur, enabling proactive troubleshooting and minimizing downtime.

6. **Scalability Monitoring:** As your application scales, it's crucial **to** have monitoring in place that can adapt. Scalability monitoring helps ensure that your application's performance remains consistent as it grows.

7. **Resource Utilization:** Monitoring resource utilization, including CPU, memory, storage, and network usage, helps identify potential performance bottlenecks and resource constraints.

8. **Log Management:** Log management tools play a vital role in tracking and analyzing application logs. They help in diagnosing issues, **tracing** transactions, and auditing security events. Efficient log management is indispensable for maintaining application health.

9. **User Experience Monitoring:** To gain a holistic view of performance, consider user experience monitoring. It involves **tracking** user interactions, load times, and overall satisfaction with your application.

10. **Dashboarding and Alerts:** - Create customized dashboards that **provide** a real-time overview of your application's performance. Set up alerts to notify you of any anomalies or critical events.

11. **Integration with DevOps Practices**: - Integrate monitoring into your DevOps processes, ensuring that performance checks are an integral part of your continuous **integration** and deployment pipelines.

In summary, the depth and breadth of your application performance monitoring strategy should align with the criticality of your application, technology stack, infrastructure, and compliance requirements. Effective monitoring and log management not only maintain the health of your application but also enable proactive responses to potential issues, ultimately improving the user experience and reducing downtime.

Continuous Monitoring For Security Events

Continuous monitoring plays a critical role in compliance and risk management. By continuously tracking and documenting security events, we can demonstrate our commitment to regulatory compliance and risk mitigation. This not only helps to avoid potential legal and financial consequences but also instills trust and confidence among our stakeholders, including clients, partners, and regulatory bodies.

In addition to these benefits, continuous monitoring facilitates threat intelligence integration. By aggregating and analyzing data from various sources, such as threat feeds, vulnerability databases, and incident reports, we can proactively identify emerging threats and trends. This insight allows us to prioritize our security efforts, allocate resources effectively and stay one step ahead of cyber adversaries. It empowers our incident response capabilities. With a well-established monitoring framework in place, we can rapidly detect and respond to security incidents, reducing the dwell time of threats within our environment. This not only limits potential damage but also enhances the ability to investigate incidents thoroughly, identify the root causes, and implement corrective actions to prevent future occurrences.

Network monitoring tools are used to continuously monitor. Datadog being one of the more popular ones to monitor an organization's entire infrastructure. There are various intrusion detection systems [IDS] and intrusion prevention systems [IPS] that are in use in conjunction, to reduce the attack surface. Depending on the network layout, IPS tools can be layered according to the needs.

Snort, Suricate, Sagan, SolarWinds are the most popular intrusion detection systems while Checkpoint, PaloAlto, Trellis are the most popular intrusion protection systems. IPS systems can be setup in multiple layers based on the desired network isolation for the organization.

In a cloud scenario, security of the VPCs in consideration is important. VPC flows logs can be routed to a cloud watch log group for alerting in AWS cloud environment.

In conclusion, continuous monitoring for security events is a cornerstone of our cybersecurity strategy. It provides us with real-time visibility, helps us assess the effectiveness of our security controls, ensures compliance, enhances threat intelligence, and strengthens our incident response capabilities. By maintaining a proactive stance through continuous monitoring, we are better equipped to safeguard our organization's assets, data, and reputation in today's ever-evolving threat landscape.

CHAPTER 10

Secrets Management and Access Control

Secret management and access control play pivotal roles in the DevOps and CI/CD (Continuous Integration/Continuous Deployment) processes, ensuring security, compliance, and smooth automation.

One major element that helps ensure security during all stages of development is proper secrets management. Securely storing, managing, and accessing sensitive information (such as passwords, API keys, certificates, and other authentication tokens) is pivotal. This involves using a combination of encryption, access controls, and other security measures to ensure that sensitive information remains secure and is only accessible to authorized machines and personnel.

Here's why they are crucial:

Security and Compliance: Secrets like passwords and API keys are sensitive gems that need protection. Secret management ensures they stay safe, complying with security standards and regulations.

Smooth Automation: Automation powers DevOps and CI/CD, and secrets are its fuel. Proper secret management keeps automation secure, letting it run smoothly without exposing valuable assets.

Data Leak Prevention: Access control stops unauthorized individuals from peeking at or tampering with secrets. This defense is vital for preventing data leaks that could lead to breaches or compliance headaches.

CI/CD Integration: CI/CD tools depend on secrets for their magic. Secret management tools seamlessly plug into these tools, providing the secrets they need during automated workflows.

Version Control Harmony: Secrets don't belong in code repositories. Secret management solutions keep secrets out of version control systems, reducing the risk of accidental exposure.

Auditing and Accountability: Good secret management offers auditing, so you can track who touched secrets and when. This accountability is vital for compliance and post-incident investigations.

In short, secret management and access control are unsung heroes in the DevOps and CI/CD story. They shield your sensitive information, fuel your automation, and keep your processes compliant. They are the guardians of agile, secure, and efficient development and deployment.

Best Practices for Managing Secrets

Integrating security initiatives at every stage of the SDLC is gaining momentum. That is, DevOps is fast evolving into a more holistic, security-first process, known as DevSecOps.

The DevSecOps approach has gained momentum recently, but teams have a long way to go when implementing its methods. A recent Ponemon study found that in 29% of organizations, security is integrated at every phase of the software development lifecycle, while at another 40%, security is integrated at some phases.

In enterprise DevOps and DevSecOps, where developers work with security and other teams in a highly connected and collaborative environment, secrets management plays a crucial role in ensuring the security and integrity of your software throughout the SDLC. It's pivotal in protecting confidential data from unauthorized access, theft, or misuse. Secrets management also lets you automate tasks like secrets rotation, dynamic injection of credentials into code, and compliance maintenance.

Conversely, ineffective secrets management can lead to serious data breaches that tarnish your company's reputation and erode customer trust. It can also result in compliance violations which invite legal penalties, fines, or even criminal charges. Not to mention, recovering from a breach is expensive, both in terms of financial costs and the time and resources required to remediate the issue.

So, as a developer, here are five best practices you must know and incorporate with your DevOps team for airtight secrets management.

1. **Enable JIT Credentials Whenever Possible**

   Just-in-Time (JIT) credentials are temporary credentials that are dynamically generated, based on the access requirements of the user or application, and automatically expire after a short period.

As JIT credentials are short-lived, there is less time for an attacker to exploit them if they are compromised. This reduces the overall attack surface and limits the damage that an attacker can cause.

In fast-paced DevOps environments where applications and infrastructure are frequently changed, long-lived credentials can create significant security risks. Issuing JIT credentials wherever possible reduces such risk to your systems and resources.

A great way to enable JIT credentials is to use Akeyless for secrets management. The tool allows DevOps teams to easily automate JIT credentials across your infrastructure, setting these secrets to expire as soon as they're used once, or as soon as a given operation is completed. The platform supports access to ephemeral objects in the CI/CD pipeline and includes out-of-the-box integrations with all major DevOps tools, ultimately helping you create a fully Zero Trust environment.

2. **Enforce Safe Password Standards**

   This is an obvious yet often overlooked aspect of secrets management because everyone thinks they're exempt. Reminding teams about using strong passwords is one thing, but setting and enforcing standards for safe passwords is another.

   Here are a few ways to do just that:

   - Create a password policy: Define a password policy that includes minimum length requirements, complexity rules, and expiration periods. Communicate this policy to all your DevOps team members.
   - Use password managers: Encourage using password managers to generate and store complex passwords. This eliminates the need to remember complex passwords and reduces the risk of password reuse.

- Implement multi-factor authentication: Use MFA wherever possible. This provides an additional layer of security by requiring users to provide multiple forms of authentication (such as by phone or email) before gaining access to critical systems.
- Monitor and audit: Use automated tools to monitor and audit password-related activities. This helps you detect and respond to security incidents quickly while reducing the risk of human error and ensuring that password standards are consistently enforced.

Consider encouraging your DevOps lead to bring a cloud-based identity and access management solution such as Okta. It's a customizable, secure, and drop-in solution to add authentication and authorization services to your applications, enabling all of the above at the organizational level.

3. **Make Sure Your Secrets Are Stored in an Encrypted Environment**

Encryption converts plaintext into ciphertext, which can only be decrypted with a secret key or password. It provides added security from unauthorized access because even if encrypted data falls into the wrong hands, it remains unreadable and unusable without the key.

If your DevOps team uses Kubernetes for orchestration, it's important to remember that the platform's native "Secrets" repository is not encrypted as a default, but rather uses base64 encoding. Moreover, even encrypted vaults can be problematic regarding decryption key governance. This is why enterprise DevOps teams often prefer to use a key management service (KMS).

A KMS generates, stores, and manages keys and provides them automatically when you need to encrypt or decrypt data. It also enables you to encrypt each dataset or resource with a different encryption key to control access at a more granular level.

With Encryption as a Service, you can encrypt data in transit and at rest. While many cloud providers offer their own encrypted vault services, these can't be used in multi-cloud DevOps environments, leading to secrets sprawl and added management workloads. Akeyless, the secrets management platform mentioned earlier, provides KMS and Encryption as a Service — which means automated encryption, rotation, and tokenization for all keys and credentials with a wide range of protocols — thus saving time and allowing your team to focus on building without compromising your security posture.

4. Monitor for Unauthorized Access

Enterprise DevOps environments comprise many moving parts: tools, teams, workflows, third-party services, etc. So, even when you follow all the best practices above, it's still possible that a breach or compromise will occur at some point.

When things go south, and an unauthorized entity gains access, it's vital to be able to monitor, detect, and respond to the incident as soon as possible to ensure minimum damage - in terms of system downtime, financial losses, and/or damage to the company's reputation.

For this, a cloud-based endpoint security platform like CrowdStrike greatly helps. It allows DevOps teams to detect and prevent unauthorized access by continuously monitoring all endpoints and alerting you about potential threats in real-time.

It uses machine learning and behavioral analytics to enable threat intelligence, vulnerability management, rapid incident response, and forensic investigation, thus providing strong protection against unauthorized access for DevOps teams.

5. **Audit Access Permissions Regularly**

Finally, as your DevOps team and its cloud infrastructure evolve over time, it's important to review who has access to which secrets regularly. This includes both human and machine identities, and the latter can often outnumber the former manyfold.

With dynamically generated credentials from your secrets management platform, it's easy to track the various identities that have accessed your vault and see in the session logs when they were approved to retrieve secrets. You get a list of all generated (system administrators, developers, third-party partners, automated services, and so forth) and their access permissions.

Then, by following the principle of least privilege, ensure any unnecessary access permissions are revoked. Timely restriction and separation of access privileges help shrink the attack surface by limiting lateral movement in the event of a breach. Ultimately, such regular audits ensure identities have access restricted precisely to what they need and are authorized for.

Secure Storage and Encryption of Secrets

Securing secrets, such as passwords and API keys, is a top priority in modern applications. Secure storage and encryption of secrets are essential for protecting sensitive information:

1. **Encryption:** Secrets are encrypted, meaning they are scrambled into unreadable formats. This ensures that even if unauthorized access occurs, the data remains protected.

2. **Secure Storage:** Secrets are stored in dedicated, highly secure repositories or vaults. Access to these repositories is tightly controlled, reducing the risk of breaches.
3. **Key Management:** Encryption keys, used to lock and unlock secrets, are managed with utmost care. They are often rotated regularly to enhance security.
4. **Zero Trust Security:** The principle of zero trust is applied, which means that even within trusted networks, secrets are treated as untrusted until proven otherwise.
5. In essence, secure storage and encryption of secrets create a robust barrier against unauthorized access, enhancing the overall security of an application or system.

Implementing Role-Based Access Control (RBAC)

Knowing how to implement RBAC is a crucial skill for building modern web applications. With an ever-increasing need to maximize security, efficiency, and usability, RBAC is an essential tool for successful app projects.

In short, role-based access control (RBAC), is a framework built around defined roles, each with associate permissions. Users are then assigned to one of these roles, to determine which actions they can take within your app.

1. **Access Control**: RBAC ensures that only authorized individuals or teams have access to specific resources or actions. This control is essential in both DevOps and DevSecOps environments to limit potential security risks.
2. **Principle of Least Privilege (PoLP):** RBAC follows the PoLP, **granting** users the minimum permissions needed to perform their tasks. This reduces the attack surface and limits the potential impact of security breaches.
3. **Workflow Efficiency**: By defining roles and permissions in a structured manner, RBAC streamlines workflows. Team members can focus on their specific responsibilities without unnecessary access to unrelated systems or data.
4. **Segregation of Duties (SoD)**: In DevSecOps, RBAC helps implement SoD by ensuring that no single user has **unchecked** access to critical security controls. This prevents conflicts of interest and promotes accountability.
5. **Compliance and Auditing**: RBAC assists in

meeting compliance requirements by clearly defining who can access **sensitive** data and perform critical actions. Auditing becomes more manageable with well-documented role assignments.

6. **Scalability**: As organizations and teams grow, RBAC scales with them. Adding new members or teams can be done seamlessly by assigning the appropriate roles and permissions.
7. **Collaboration**: In DevOps and DevSecOps, collaboration is key. RBAC facilitates collaboration by allowing teams to work together on projects while maintaining control over who can make changes or access resources.
8. **Security Automation**: Automation tools and scripts can be integrated with RBAC to enforce security policies and access controls consistently throughout the DevOps pipeline.

Some of the key examples of RBAC implementation in DevOps are as follows:

1. **Git Repositories**:
   - Define roles such as "Developers," "QA

Testers," and "Admins."

- Assign read-only access to Developers for source code repositories.
- Allow QA Testers to create branches and merge code to a staging branch.
- Reserve administrative privileges for Admins, who can manage users, repositories, and access permissions.

2. **CI/CD Pipelines:**
   - Create roles like "Build Engineers," "Deployment Managers," and "Auditors."
   - Give Build Engineers permission to configure and run build jobs.
   - Allow Deployment Managers to deploy applications to production environments.
   - Grant Auditors read-only access to view pipeline configurations and logs for auditing purposes.

3. **Cloud Infrastructure**:
   - Use RBAC features provided by cloud providers (e.g., AWS IAM, Azure RBAC).

- Define roles like "Infrastructure Admin," "Database Operator," and "Security Analyst."
- Assign permissions based on responsibilities; Infrastructure Admins can provision resources, Database Operators can manage databases, and Security Analysts can monitor security configurations.

4. **Security Tools:**
    - In DevSecOps, RBAC is crucial for security tools like vulnerability scanners.
    - Create roles such as "Security Analysts," "DevOps Engineers," and "Security Admins."
    - Allow Security Analysts to run scans and view reports.
    - DevOps Engineers can trigger scans but not access sensitive scan results.
    - Reserve administrative control for Security Admins who configure scan policies and manage user access.

5. **Access to Sensitive Data:**
    - Protect access to sensitive data repositories

(e.g., databases, secret stores).

- Define roles like "Data Scientists," "Database Administrators," and "Data Auditors."
- Limit access to data based on job requirements; Data Scientists can query data, DB Administrators can manage databases, and Data Auditors can review data access logs.

6. **Incident Response:**
   - During security incidents, RBAC helps control actions.
   - Assign roles such as "Incident Responders," "Forensic Analysts," and "Incident Coordinators."
   - Incident Responders can gather data and initiate actions.
   - Forensic Analysts have access to investigation tools.
   - Incident Coordinators oversee the response, including communication with stakeholders.

7. **Compliance Monitoring**:

- RBAC assists in ensuring compliance with industry standards (e.g., PCI DSS, HIPAA).
- Create roles such as "Compliance Managers" and "Compliance Auditors."
- Compliance Managers define and enforce policies.
- Compliance Auditors review configurations and reports to verify compliance.

These examples illustrate how RBAC can be tailored to various DevOps and DevSecOps scenarios. By defining roles and assigning appropriate permissions, organizations can enhance security, streamline operations, and maintain compliance throughout their software development and deployment processes.

Securing Credentials in CI/CD Pipelines

Over the past six months, we've listened to hundreds of engineers share their pain and challenges for managing secrets while delivering with CI/CD pipelines. Below are the most common features requested of software delivery platforms:

- A central place to see all the secrets that are used within CD tools. .
- Fine-grained access management for each secret.
- Visibility into secrets usage across deployment workflows and pipelines, e.g., ssh key being used in workflow X.
- Changelog capabilities to track when was the secret added, by who, and what changed.
- Notifications when a secret is used at runtime (e.g., Jenkins password being used to download artifacts or SSH key being used to deploy the artifact to a server).
- Deprecate and remove outdated secrets - implement secrets rotation.
- Migrate existing secrets to a new service, e.g., moving secrets to a different Vault setup or a different Amazon KMS.
- Deactivate the secret at KMS or Vault level in case there is a threat of compromise.

To achieve this, avoid hardcoding credentials directly into pipeline scripts and instead rely on secure environment variables provided by your CI/CD platform. Employ dedicated secret management tools to store and control access to secrets, ensuring encryption both at rest and in transit. Implement strict access control mechanisms, such as RBAC, to restrict who can access and modify secret variables within the CI/CD environment. Prevent secrets from being stored in code repositories and leverage features that mask or redact secrets in logs and outputs. Regularly rotate credentials, and use short-lived or temporary credentials whenever possible. Auditing and monitoring tools can help track and respond to any unauthorized access or modifications. By adhering to these practices, you can fortify your CI/CD pipelines against credential exposure and potential security breaches.

Secrets Storage and Management Tools

Secrets management systems offer solutions for storing and accessing secrets. Popular solutions include HashiCorp's Vault, Docker Secrets, KeyWhiz, and AWS Secrets Manager. It's fairly common now that secrets management tools offer not only secret storage, but also key management/encryption and identity management (this is where we hear about services like AWS KMS and PKI as a service, respectively). Let's discuss HashiCorp Vault and Amazon KMS in more detail.

HashiCorp Vault

HashiCorp's Vault is a commonly used open-source solution for storing and managing secrets. The stored data is encrypted, and access to that data is shared with tokens. These tokens can be created using specific privileges for specific lease times giving access to specific secrets. The tokens can be revoked at any time, making the secrets inaccessible.

It's a popular way of centralizing sensitive data.

Every component of your delivery architecture that uses secrets accesses them at runtime via access tokens and discards them immediately, making sure that secrets access is never available for longer than needed.

Amazon KMS

Amazon KMS is a popular solution for encrypting and decrypting secrets. Using Amazon KMS, users create an encryption key assigned an Amazon IAM role, which is configured to share the level of access for services, environments, machines, and any other component in our architecture, including CI and CD systems. This key reference is used for encryption and decryption.

To gain a better understanding of how key management systems work, here are the steps involved with encryption/decryption.

- During data encryption, a new encryption key is asked from KMS, which returns the key and the key's encrypted value.
- Using the plain text key, the secret is encrypted.
- The encrypted key and encrypted secret then are

stored.

- For decryption, the encrypted key is sent to KMS, which in turn returns the plaintext key.
- Using the plain text key, the secret is then decrypted and used.

This ensures that sensitive information is never stored in a system as plaintext data (key or value), and that for each secret that gets stored, the encryption key is unique. The capability for encryption/decryption of keys can be controlled through the AWS console, and if there's ever a breach, the master key can be disabled, ensuring no one gets further access using the exposed secret.

CHAPTER 11

Continuous Security Testing

Continuous Security Testing is a crucial practice in the world of DevSecOps, where security is integrated seamlessly into the software development and deployment pipeline. This chapter delves into various aspects of continuous security testing, including dynamic application security testing (DAST), security scanning for containerized environments, fuzz testing, and security test automation. It emphasizes the importance of identifying and addressing security vulnerabilities at every stage of the development lifecycle. Readers will learn how to integrate security testing into the CI/CD pipeline, automating the detection of security flaws early in the development process. Real-world examples and case studies provide insights into how organizations can bolster their security posture and respond proactively to evolving threats.

Integrating Security Testing Into CI/CD Pipeline

Integrating security testing into the CI/CD (Continuous Integration/Continuous Deployment) pipeline is a fundamental step in achieving a robust DevSecOps environment. This practice ensures that security checks are automated and continuously applied throughout the software development lifecycle, from code creation to deployment.

1. **Early Detection of Vulnerabilities:** By incorporating security testing tools and practices into CI/CD pipelines, vulnerabilities can be identified at their inception. This early detection is critical for addressing security flaws before they propagate further into the development process.

2. **Automated Scanning**: Security testing tools automate the scanning of code and infrastructure components, checking for known vulnerabilities, misconfigurations, and compliance violations. These scans occur automatically with each code commit or deployment, saving time and effort.

3. **Vulnerability Prioritization**: Security tools provide insights into the severity of vulnerabilities, allowing teams to prioritize and remediate the most critical issues first. This data-driven approach ensures that security efforts are focused where they are needed most.

4. **Continuous Feedback**: Security testing in CI/CD pipelines provides continuous feedback to developers and operations teams. When a vulnerability is detected, feedback is immediate, allowing developers to fix issues quickly and efficiently.

5. **Security as Code**: Integrating security into code repositories and infrastructure configurations, known as "Security as Code," ensures that security policies are enforced automatically. This minimizes the risk of configuration drift and security policy violations.

6. **Shift Left Security**: This practice encourages "shifting left" security, meaning that security considerations are brought earlier into the development process. Developers become more security-aware, reducing the likelihood of introducing vulnerabilities in the first place.

7. **Compliance and Reporting**: CI/CD pipelines with security testing capabilities provide compliance reports, demonstrating adherence to security standards and regulatory requirements. This is crucial for audits and certifications.

8. **Remediation Automation**: Some security testing tools can automatically trigger remediation actions, such as quarantining vulnerable components or rolling back deployments when critical issues are identified.

9. **Third-Party Component Scanning**: In addition to code, security testing can extend to scanning third-party libraries and dependencies, which are common attack vectors for cyber threats.

Integrating security testing into the CI/CD pipeline is a proactive and efficient approach to ensure that software is not only functional but also secure. It aligns with the principles of DevSecOps, where security is not a separate phase but an integral part of the development and deployment process, enhancing the overall security posture of applications and systems.

Example: Integrating OWASP ZAP with Jenkins for CI/CD Security Testing

One effective way to integrate security testing into a CI/CD pipeline is by using the OWASP ZAP (Zed Attack Proxy) tool along with Jenkins, a popular automation server. Here's a simplified example of how this integration works:

1. **Jenkins Setup:**
   - Set up a Jenkins pipeline that automates the build and deployment process of your application.

2. **Security Testing Stage:**
    - Introduce a dedicated stage in your Jenkins pipeline for security testing. This stage is where OWASP ZAP will come into play.

3. **OWASP ZAP Configuration:**
    - Configure OWASP ZAP to scan your application for security vulnerabilities. You can define scan policies, authentication settings, and target URLs within the OWASP ZAP configuration.
4. **Execute OWASP ZAP:**
    - In your Jenkins pipeline, trigger OWASP ZAP to run security scans on your application as part of the security testing stage.

5. **Scan Results:**
    - OWASP ZAP will perform scans, identifying security vulnerabilities like SQL injection, cross-site scripting (XSS), and more. It generates detailed reports with findings.

6. **Reporting and Alerts:**
   - Set up Jenkins to process OWASP ZAP's scan reports. You can generate alerts or notifications when critical vulnerabilities are detected.

7. **Fail the Build (if needed):**
   - Optionally, you can configure your Jenkins pipeline to fail the build if certain high-severity vulnerabilities are identified, ensuring that insecure code doesn't progress further in the pipeline.

8. **Remediation and Feedback:**
   - Developers receive immediate feedback on security issues, allowing them to address vulnerabilities promptly. They can then commit fixes to the codebase.

9. **Continuous Integration:**

- This security testing stage becomes an integral part of your CI/CD pipeline, ensuring that security checks are performed automatically with every code commit and deployment.

In this example, OWASP ZAP is used to automate security scans within a Jenkins CI/CD pipeline. However, various other security testing tools, such as Burp Suite, SonarQube, or Checkmarx, can also be integrated similarly, depending on your specific requirements and tool preferences. The goal is to incorporate security checks seamlessly into your pipeline, providing continuous security assessment of your applications as they progress from development to deployment.

Dynamic Application Security Testing (DAST)

Dynamic Application Security Testing (DAST) is a critical component of continuous security testing, focusing on identifying vulnerabilities in running applications by simulating real-world attacks. In this section, we delve into the principles and practices of DAST:

1. **Realistic Testing**: DAST evaluates applications in their live, running state, providing a real-world perspective of potential vulnerabilities. It mimics how attackers would interact with the application.

2. **Black-Box Testing**: DAST is often considered a "black-box" testing method, as it assesses the application from an external perspective, without knowledge of its internal code or architecture.

3. **Vulnerability Scanning**: DAST tools scan applications for a wide range of vulnerabilities, including SQL injection, cross-site scripting (XSS), security misconfigurations, and more. They send various HTTP requests to the application to identify weaknesses.
4. **Continuous Scanning**: DAST can be integrated into CI/CD pipelines, enabling continuous scanning of applications as they evolve. This ensures that new vulnerabilities are promptly identified and addressed.

5. **Automated Exploration**: DAST tools automatically explore an application's attack surface, probing for vulnerabilities across different parts of the application, such as web forms, APIs, and authentication mechanisms.

6. **Reporting**: DAST generates detailed reports highlighting identified vulnerabilities, their severity, and potential impact. These reports aid in prioritizing and remediating issues.

7. **False Positives**: DAST tools may produce false-positive findings, so it's essential to validate and verify each reported vulnerability to ensure accuracy.

8. **Compliance**: DAST helps organizations meet compliance requirements by actively testing applications for security flaws and demonstrating due diligence in addressing vulnerabilities.

9. **Web Application Firewalls (WAF):** DAST

results can be used to fine-tune Web Application Firewalls (WAFs) to provide additional protection against known vulnerabilities.

10. **Integrations**: DAST tools can integrate with CI/CD pipelines, issue tracking systems, and security orchestration platforms, streamlining the vulnerability management process.

In this section, readers will gain insights into how DAST complements other security testing methods and contributes to a holistic security posture. By the end, they will understand how DAST empowers organizations to proactively discover and address vulnerabilities in their web applications, reducing the risk of exploitation by malicious actors.

Security Scanning for Containerized Environments

Are your container and Docker image secure?

Let's find out!

Hackers have gone very active in the past few years. Even big organizations like Facebook, Google, and Yahoo have been victims to attacks losing millions of dollars. That is why an application's security is the utmost important thing in every organization today.

Many of these applications today run inside containers as they are easily scalable, cost-effective, faster deployable, take lesser storage, and use resources far better than virtual machines. So, the security factor of these containers is very crucial. A container image is made up of layers, and to get a real understanding of an image's vulnerability stance, you need to access each layer. The smaller container images have a lesser chance to get exposed to potential vulnerabilities.

Containerization is one of the core stages in the DevOps process where security must be looked at on a serious note. A container image can have many bugs and security vulnerabilities, which gives a good opportunity for hackers to get access to the application or data present on the container costing millions to the company.

Hence, it is crucial to scan and audit the images and containers regularly. DevSecOps plays an important role in adding security to the DevOps processes, including scanning images and containers for bugs and vulnerabilities.

A container security scanner will help you find all the vulnerabilities inside your containers and monitor them regularly against any attack, issue, or a new bug.

Let's explore the available options.

1. **Clair :** Clair is an open-source project which offers static security and vulnerability scanning for docker and application (appc) containers. It is an API-driven analysis engine that checks for security flaws in the containers layer by layer. You can build services using Clair, which can monitor your containers continuously for any

container vulnerabilities. It notifies you about a potential threat in the container. It notifies you about a potential threat in the container based on the Common Vulnerabilities and Exposures database (CVE) and similar databases. If any threat or issue identifies which is already there in the National Vulnerability Database (NVD), it will retrieve the details and provide the details in the report.

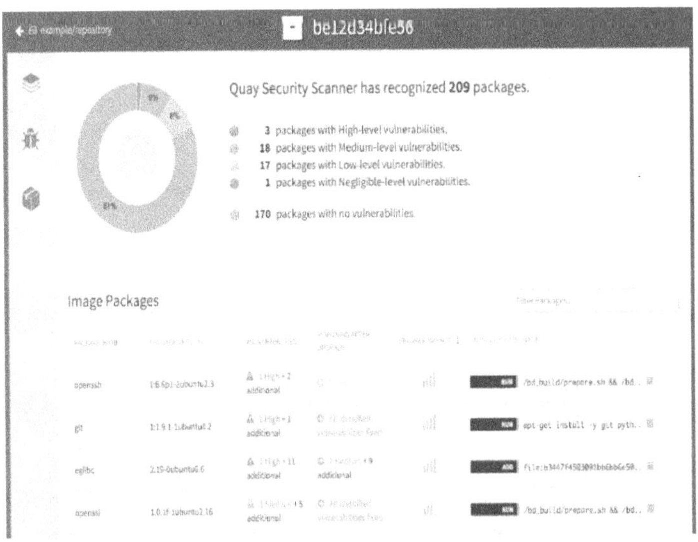

2. **Anchore:** Anchore Engine is an open-source tool for scanning container images and Helm charts. It provides detailed vulnerability reports, policy

checks, and compliance assessments, empowering organizations to enforce security policies and ensure secure container deployments.

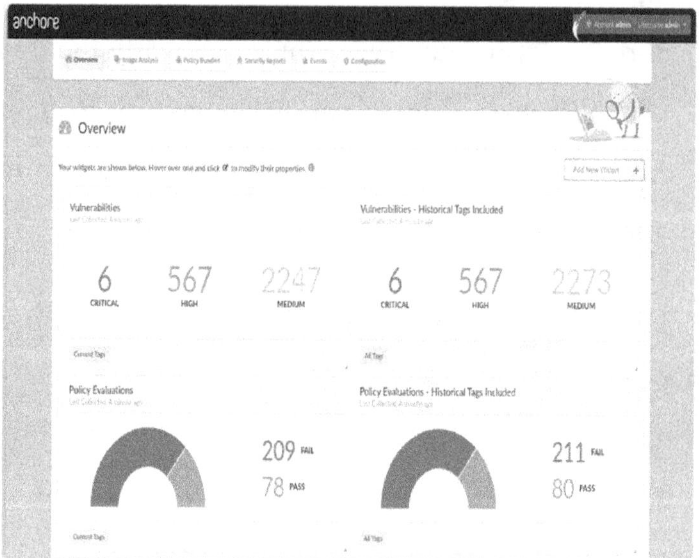

3. **Aqua Security:** Aqua Security provides a comprehensive container security platform that includes vulnerability scanning. It not only scans images but also monitors container runtime environments, ensuring end-to-end container security. Aqua helps organizations protect their containerized applications against vulnerabilities

and runtime threats.

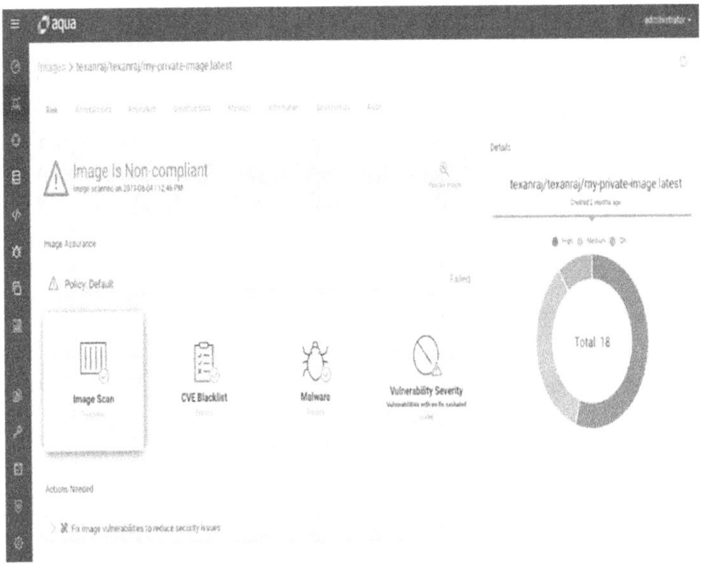

Common Container Vulnerabilities

Containerized applications can include a wide variety of different vulnerabilities. Some of the most common types include the following:

- **Application Vulnerabilities:** The applications running within a container may contain vulnerabilities. For example, a web application may include an SQL injection or buffer overflow vulnerability that leaves it vulnerable to attack.

- **Insecure Configurations:** In addition to potential vulnerabilities in their code, applications can also have security issues introduced by misconfigurations. For example, an optional setting in an application, if enabled, may allow an access control bypass or use of an insecure protocol.
- **Network Threats:** Containerized applications have the ability to communicate with other systems via the network. If these network communications are not configured securely, there is the potential for eavesdropping or exploitation of the containerized application.
- **Access Control Issues:** Like other applications and systems, containerized applications should have access controls in place to manage access to the application and any sensitive functionality or data. Overly permissive access controls could enable data breaches, malware infections, or other threats.

What Types of Container Vulnerabilities Can Be Detected?

Container scanning can identify a wide range of potential issues with a container. Some common examples include the following:

- **Image Vulnerabilities:** A container image vulnerability is a vulnerability with the image embedded within a container. For example, a container image may include an insecure library or dependency that is used by the base image.
- **Malicious Images:** Containers are often built based on third-party images. An image from an untrusted source may include malware or security misconfigurations designed to make containers built using it vulnerable to attack.
- **Access Controls:** Containers have built-in access controls to limit users' access to the container itself. If these access controls are misconfigured or vulnerable, an attacker may be able to escalate their privileges and take over the container.
- **Application Vulnerabilities:** The applications installed within a container can include vulnerabilities that make them vulnerable to

attack

Fuzz Testing and Security Test Automations

Fuzz Testing and Security Test Automation: Advancing Security Protocols

In the realm of continuous security testing, Fuzz Testing and Security Test Automation stand as innovative practices:

1. **Fuzz Testing (Fuzzing)**: Fuzz testing involves subjecting software systems to a barrage of unexpected, malformed, or random inputs to discover vulnerabilities and flaws. It simulates real-world scenarios where attackers attempt to manipulate input data. Fuzzing can uncover critical vulnerabilities like buffer overflows, input validation issues, and other unexpected

software behaviors that might lead to security breaches. Automation plays a crucial role in scaling fuzz testing to assess various application components systematically.

2. **Security Test Automation**: Security Test Automation extends beyond traditional testing methods by employing automated tools and scripts to continuously evaluate the security posture of applications and infrastructure. This approach covers a wide range of security assessments, including vulnerability scanning, penetration testing, and compliance checks. Security Test Automation integrates seamlessly into CI/CD pipelines, ensuring that security assessments occur continuously and consistently throughout the software development lifecycle.

This section delves into the techniques, tools, and practices associated with Fuzz Testing and Security Test Automation. Readers will discover how these methodologies enhance security by uncovering vulnerabilities, automating security assessments, and providing early insights into potential threats, ultimately bolstering the resilience of modern software systems against evolving security challenges.

CHAPTER 12

Security Governance in DevOps

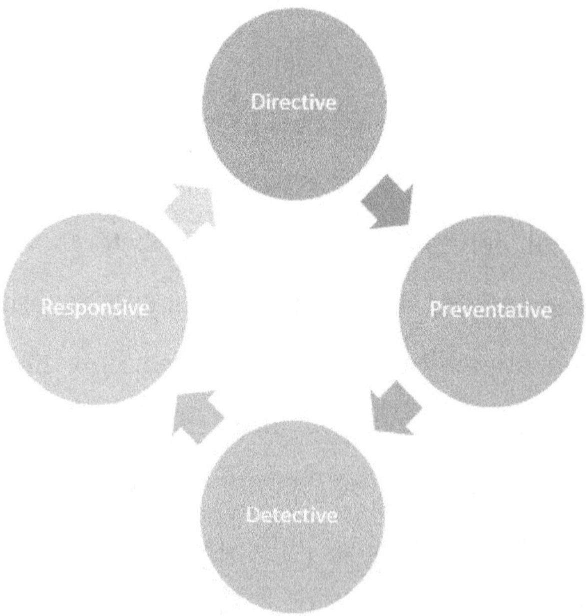

The chapter on "Security Governance in DevOps" dives into the critical role that governance frameworks and practices play in ensuring robust security within DevOps environments:

1. **Establishing Security Governance Frameworks**: DevOps teams are tasked with implementing security governance frameworks that define the rules, policies, and procedures for securing the development and deployment pipelines. These frameworks provide a structured approach to managing security across the entire DevOps ecosystem.

2. **Security Policies and Standards**: The chapter explores the creation and enforcement of security policies and standards tailored to DevOps processes. These policies align with industry best practices and regulatory requirements, ensuring that security remains at the forefront of every development and deployment decision.

2. **Security Awareness and Training Programs**: Effective security governance includes initiatives to educate and raise awareness among DevOps teams. The chapter discusses the importance of security training programs, which empower team members to understand and address security concerns proactively.

3. **Security Metrics and Key Performance Indicators (KPIs):** Measuring security effectiveness is vital. Readers will learn how to define and track security metrics and KPIs that provide insights into the success of security governance efforts. These metrics aid in making data-driven decisions to improve security practices.

By the end of this chapter, readers will have a comprehensive understanding of how to establish and maintain security governance in DevOps, ensuring that security controls are well-defined, policies are enforced, and teams are equipped with the knowledge and tools needed to navigate the security landscape effectively.

Establishing Security Governance Frameworks

Establishing security governance frameworks in DevOps is essential for ensuring that security remains a central focus throughout the software development and delivery process. Here's an overview of how it's done:

1. **Define Security Policies and Standards:** Start by defining clear and concise security policies and standards that align with industry best practices and compliance requirements. These policies should cover areas like data protection, access control, code reviews, vulnerability management, and incident response.

2. **Create Security Governance Boards:** Establish cross-functional security governance boards that include representatives from development,

operations, security, and compliance teams. These boards are responsible for reviewing and approving security policies, standards, and changes to the DevOps environment.

2. **Implement Security as Code (SaC):** Embed security controls directly into the DevOps pipeline using the concept of Security as Code (SaC). This involves writing security policies and checks as code and integrating them into the CI/CD process. For example, use tools like HashiCorp Sentinel or Open Policy Agent (OPA) to enforce policies on infrastructure code.

3. **Develop Compliance Templates**: Create compliance templates that define security and compliance requirements as code. Tools like AWS CloudFormation StackSets or Terraform Enterprise can be used to automate the deployment of compliant infrastructure across multiple environments

.

4. **Continuous Monitoring**: Implement continuous monitoring tools and practices to assess the security posture of your DevOps environment in

real-time. Tools like Prometheus, Grafana, or commercial solutions like Datadog can help monitor infrastructure and application metrics, security events, and anomalies.

5. **Security Review Pipelines**: Incorporate security review pipelines into your CI/CD process. These pipelines include security checks, vulnerability scanning, and compliance assessments. When code is committed, it goes through these automated checks, ensuring that security standards are met before deployment.

6. **Audit Trails and Logging:** Establish comprehensive audit trails and logging practices to track changes and access to critical systems. Centralized log management and analysis tools like the Elastic Stack (ELK) can help in this regard.

7. **Diagrams and Documentation:** Use visual diagrams and documentation to illustrate the flow of security controls within your DevOps

environment. Diagrams can be created using tools like draw.io or Lucidchart. They provide a clear overview of how security is integrated into each stage of the pipeline.

8. **Compliance Frameworks:** Leverage compliance frameworks like CIS (Center for Internet Security) benchmarks or NIST (National Institute of Standards and Technology) guidelines to guide your security governance efforts. These frameworks provide detailed recommendations for securing various aspects of your DevOps ecosystem

Useful Link:
https://www.cncf.io/blog/2022/10/14/securing-ci-cd-pipelines-through-security-gates-with-kubescape/

Security Policies and Standards for DevOps

Security policies and standards are the backbone of a robust security governance framework in DevOps. They provide clear guidelines and rules for protecting critical assets and ensuring compliance with industry regulations and best practices. Here's an overview of essential security policies and standards for DevOps:

1. **Access Control Policy:**
    - Define who has access to what resources in your DevOps environment.
    - Specify role-based access control (RBAC)

and permissions for teams and individuals.

- Implement multi-factor authentication (MFA) where necessary.

2. **Data Encryption Standard:**
    - Specify encryption standards for data at rest and in transit.
    - Define encryption algorithms and key management practices.
    - Ensure encryption is applied to sensitive data, including user credentials and customer information.
3. **Incident Response Plan:**
    - Develop a detailed incident response plan that outlines steps to take in case of a security breach or incident.
    - Assign roles and responsibilities for incident response team members.
    - Include communication procedures, mitigation strategies, and post-incident analysis.

4. **Vulnerability Management Policy:**
    - Establish a process for identifying,

prioritizing, and remedying vulnerabilities in software and infrastructure.

- Define how often vulnerability assessments should be conducted.
- Outline procedures for patch management and vulnerability remediation.

5. **Code Review and Secure Coding Standards:**
   - Set coding standards and best practices for secure software development.
   - Specify code review procedures, including the use of static code analysis tools.
   - Promote secure coding practices such as input validation, escaping, and avoiding common vulnerabilities (e.g., SQL injection, XSS).

6. **Compliance with Regulatory Standards:**
   - Identify relevant regulatory requirements (e.g., GDPR, HIPAA, PCI DSS) for your industry and region.
   - Develop policies and practices to ensure compliance with these standards.
   - Conduct regular audits and assessments to

validate compliance.

7. **Change Management Policy:**
    - Define how changes to the DevOps environment, including infrastructure and code, should be managed.
    - Implement a change approval process to review and authorize changes before deployment.
    - Ensure rollback procedures are in place in case of unsuccessful changes.

8. **Data Retention and Destruction Policy:**
    - Specify data retention periods and practices.
    - Define procedures for securely destroying data when it is no longer needed.
    - Ensure compliance with data privacy regulations regarding data retention and deletion.

9. **Security Awareness and Training:**
    - Outline a training program to educate DevOps

team members about security best practices and policies.

- Promote a culture of security awareness and continuous learning.
- Include phishing awareness training to prevent social engineering attacks.

10. **Cloud Security Standards (if applicable):**
    - If using cloud services, define security standards and configurations specific to the chosen cloud provider.
    - Specify how cloud resources should be provisioned, configured, and monitored securely.

These policies and standards serve as the foundation for a secure DevOps environment. They guide teams in making security-conscious decisions, implementing controls, and adhering to best practices throughout the software development lifecycle. Regular reviews and updates to these policies ensure that security remains effective and aligned with evolving threats and technologies.

Use Case: Secure Deployment of a Financial Application

Background: A financial services company is developing a customer-facing web application for online banking. Given the sensitivity of financial data and the need to comply with financial regulations, the company is committed to ensuring the security and compliance of their DevOps pipeline.

Application Components:

- Web application codebase
- Containerized microservices
- Kubernetes-based orchestration
- Cloud-based infrastructure
- Continuous Integration/Continuous Deployment (CI/CD) pipeline

In the above financial application deployment you can apply these policies and there are more use cases where it will be applicable.

Security Awareness and Training Programs

Security awareness and training programs play a crucial role in educating DevOps teams about security best practices and ensuring a culture of security within organizations. Here are some key security awareness and training programs and resources that are commonly used in DevOps environments:

1. **OWASP Top Ten**: The Open Web Application Security Project (OWASP) provides resources, training materials, and online courses to educate developers and security professionals about the top web application security risks. The "OWASP Top Ten" is a widely recognized resource for understanding common vulnerabilities.

2. **SANS Institute**: The SANS Institute offers a variety of cybersecurity training courses and certifications, including those focused on secure coding, incident response, and penetration testing. Their courses are well-regarded in the industry.
3. **(ISC)²**: The International Information System Security Certification Consortium, or (ISC)², provides certifications such as Certified Information Systems Security Professional (CISSP) and Certified Secure Software Lifecycle

Professional (CSSLP) that are valuable for individuals involved in DevOps and security.

4. **NIST Cybersecurity Framework**: The National Institute of Standards and Technology (NIST) offers resources and training materials related to their Cybersecurity Framework, which provides guidelines for improving cybersecurity practices. This framework is widely adopted by organizations.

5. **Security Training by Cloud Providers**: Cloud service providers like AWS, Azure, and Google Cloud offer security training resources and certifications specific to their platforms. These resources can be valuable for DevOps professionals working in cloud environments.

6. **DevSecOps Certification Programs**: Various organizations and training providers offer DevSecOps certification programs designed to equip individuals with the knowledge and skills

to integrate security into DevOps processes effectively.

7. **Secure Coding Training**: Many training programs focus on secure coding practices, including language-specific training for programming languages commonly used in DevOps, such as Python, JavaScript, Java, and others.

8. **Online Learning Platforms**: Platforms like Udemy, Coursera, edX, and Pluralsight offer a wide range of cybersecurity and DevSecOps courses, making it easy for individuals to access training from anywhere.

9. **Security Conferences and Webinars**: Attending security conferences and webinars allows DevOps professionals to stay up-to-date with the latest security trends, best practices, and emerging threats.

When implementing a security awareness and training program in a DevOps environment, organizations often tailor their approach to address their specific needs and technologies. Combining a mix of these resources and programs can help DevOps teams stay informed about security and build the skills needed to integrate security effectively into their workflows

Security Metrics and Key Performance Indicators (KPIs)

Security metrics and key performance indicators (KPIs) are essential for assessing the effectiveness of security practices and for making informed decisions in DevOps environments. Here are some common security metrics and KPIs used to gauge the security posture of DevOps processes and systems:

1. **Vulnerability Density**: This metric calculates the number of vulnerabilities per unit of code, typically per thousand lines of code (KLOC). It helps assess the quality of code and identify areas with a high concentration of vulnerabilities.
2. **Vulnerability Remediation Rate**: It measures the speed at which vulnerabilities are remediated or patched after discovery. A higher remediation rate indicates a more efficient response to security vulnerabilities.

3. **Incident Response Time**: This KPI tracks the time taken to detect and respond to security incidents. Shorter incident response times

indicate a more effective incident management process.

4. **Change Success Rate**: This metric assesses the percentage of changes or deployments that are completed successfully without causing security incidents or disruptions. A higher change success rate indicates better change management practices.

5. **Security Awareness Score**: It measures the security awareness of DevOps team members based on their performance in security training and awareness programs. A high awareness score indicates a security-conscious workforce.

These metrics and KPIs provide valuable insights into the security posture of DevOps processes and systems. They enable organizations to identify areas that require improvement, demonstrate the effectiveness of security measures, and make data-driven decisions to enhance security practices.

CHAPTER 13

Compliance Automation

Automating Compliance Checks and

Audits

Automating compliance checks and audits in DevOps involves using tools and processes to continuously monitor, assess, and enforce compliance with security policies, regulatory requirements, and industry standards. This approach enhances security, streamlines audits, and reduces manual effort. Key elements include:

1. **Continuous Monitoring**: Employ automated tools to continuously monitor infrastructure, code, and configurations for compliance violations and vulnerabilities.

2. **Policy as Code**: Define security policies and standards as code, integrating them into the DevOps pipeline to ensure real-time compliance checks.

3. **Audit Trails**: Maintain detailed audit logs of all changes and security events, facilitating compliance audits and investigations.

4. **Automated Reporting**: Generate automated compliance reports and dashboards to provide stakeholders with real-time visibility into compliance status.

5. **Alerting and Remediation**: Implement automated alerting for compliance violations and integrate remediation processes to address issues promptly.

6. **Integration with CI/CD**: Embed compliance checks into the CI/CD pipeline to prevent non-compliant code or configurations from progressing.

By automating compliance checks and audits, DevOps teams can ensure that security and compliance are intrinsic to their processes, reducing the risk of security breaches and simplifying the audit process.

Example:

```
pipeline {
  agent any

  stages {
    stage('Code Commit') {
      steps {
        // Your code checkout and repository
setup here
      }
    }

    stage('Code Build (CI)') {
      steps {
        // Build your code, run unit tests, and
perform static code analysis
        // Example:
        sh 'mvn clean install'
      }
    }
        stage('Security Compliance Check') {
```

```
            steps {
                // Run automated security compliance
checks based on policies as code
                // Example: Use a tool like AWS Config to
check AWS resource configurations
                // Ensure that security policies are
enforced as code
                // Example:
                sh 'aws configservice put-config-rule --
config-rule-name my-security-rule --input-
parameters
"{\"sourceIdentifier\":\"AWS::::Account\"}"'
            }
        }

        stage('Automated Testing') {
            steps {
                // Deploy the application to a test
environment
                // Run automated functional, integration,
and security tests
                // Example:
                sh 'deploy-test-environment.sh'
                sh 'run-automated-tests.sh'
```

```
        }
      }
          stage('Deployment (CD)') {
        steps {
          // Deploy the application to a staging
environment
          // Use infrastructure as code (IaC)
templates for provisioning
          // Example:
          sh 'deploy-staging-environment.sh'
        }
      }

      stage('Dynamic Application Security Testing
(DAST)') {
        steps {
          // Run dynamic application security
testing (DAST) tools
```

Implementing Continuous Compliance Monitoring

Modern organizations deal with large volumes of sensitive user data, which makes compliance management a must for building customer trust and avoiding hefty fines. Making last-minute security maneuvers whenever the date for compliance audit approaches or a cyber attack happens, is not good for the organization in the long run.

Continuous compliance is a must for achieving and maintaining compliance with industry and regulatory requirements in any organization on an ongoing basis.

What is Continuous Compliance ?

Before getting into details on continuous compliance, we need to first understand what compliance is. Compliance is defined as the state of being in accordance with established guidelines or specifications or the process of becoming so.

For example, while developing software code, it should be developed in compliance with specifications created by a standards body, and deployed by user organizations in compliance with the vendor's licensing agreement. The regulations and standards for compliance are different in every industry. Workplace compliance is the act of complying with federal, state, or local laws and regulations.

There are two main types of compliance –

1. Corporate
2. Regulatory

Both these types comprise a framework of rules, regulations, and practices to follow. Corporate compliance refers to the rules and regulations that an organization puts into place for compliance with both external and internal policies. Regulatory compliance on the other hand applies to the rules and regulations an organization puts into place for compliance with external regulations.

Compliance must not be considered as a one-off event, but an ongoing practice that every business has to follow at all times. Continuous compliance is achieving compliance with regulatory requirements, industry standards, and best practices across your IT and business environment and then maintaining it on an ongoing basis.

Continuous compliance helps develop and incorporate a strategy in the organization that continually monitors your compliance position. This way, you can stay updated on your compliance requirements instead of reviewing them with an annual audit alone or when a non-compliance event occurs.

Continuous compliance ensures security across the organization by notifying teams of non-compliance issues in real time. Continuous compliance monitoring is a continuous approach to identifying non-compliant endpoints in your infrastructure without waiting for periodic audits and causing security gaps.

Continuous compliance is not a one-size-fits-all solution. It branches into different facets or processes that you need to proactively undertake based on your compliance requirements and company security requirements.

- Vulnerability management – The process of finding all the vulnerabilities within a given system, determining their importance, fixing the issues, and documenting the entire process, is called vulnerability management.
- Policy management – Internal rules, company best practices, and federal laws are part of policy management.
- Vendor management – Monitoring the privacy practices of third-party vendors is part of vendor management.
- Data management – The process of managing your data to keep it secure is referred to as data

management.

- Risk management – All the efforts towards implementing a risk strategy, identifying risk types, and categorizing them by priority, are part of the risk management policy.
- Incident management – Handling any type of hardware or software failures, cyber-attacks, or malware attacks is considered incident management.
- HR management – Applying compliance policies to create a better working environment for employees and risk-averse businesses is part of HR management.

Continuous compliance eliminates response delays whenever a compliance issue arises. The organization needs to build a framework as a starting point and then expand from there.

How can Continuous Compliance help organizations?

A report by Ponemon Institute reveals that the cost of non-compliance is 2.71 times higher than the cost of compliance. The study breaks down this cost into business disruption, productivity losses, revenue losses, and penalties or settlement costs. While revenue loss is the biggest motivating factor that drives businesses to implement a security-first approach, continuous compliance has many benefits.

Passing audit checks is a major apprehension that requires a lot of manual effort like figuring out specific requirements, documenting, fixing gaps, and more. However, traditional processes don't always meet the required level of efficiency, leading to piled-up tasks and little time till the deadline. This creates a gap between the actual and desired level of compliance.

As the gap keeps growing till the next audit cycle, closing it becomes a costly challenge. Even organizations that passed their audit check tend to fall out of compliance once certified. Continuous compliance bridges the gap between the desired level of compliance during a pre-audit stage and the actual or achieved level.

Continuous compliance also provides real-time

visibility into the complex IT infrastructure and helps address gaps as soon as it surfaces. If delayed, the gaps tend to affect multiple connected systems and cause costly damages. Most businesses don't prioritize fixing their security gaps until an incident occurs. However, SaaS providers are changing this mindset as they know the repercussions of data loss and are left with little choice to set up a continuous compliance process.

Pros and Cons of Continuous Compliance:

Before going in for a continuous compliance solution, it would be a good thing to know the pros and cons of implementing continuous compliance solutions. The pros of continuous compliance are listed below –

Frequent And Quick Security Checks

Continuous compliance solutions install health checks as the primary control process for maintaining compliance at all times. A compliance management solution helps process owners to conduct frequent and fast compliance checks and respond proactively to vulnerabilities and compliance gaps.

Minimizes Human Error

Errors and inconsistencies are common when teams manually process large volumes of data using spreadsheets. Continuous compliance eliminates the burden of the entire compliance management from IT teams and reduces the risk of compliance error.

Provides Deeper Visibility

Manual compliance management lacks visibility and transparency into compliance statuses. The visibility of an automated compliance solution eliminates the scramble to dig for information for compliance audits. It provides complete visibility into the security state of servers, compliance policies, and regulatory changes.

Design Compliance

While building applications it is important to adhere

to compliance and security policies throughout the app development lifecycle. A continuous compliance process ensures that app development is in sync with compliance requirements at all stage

The cons of Continuous Compliance listed below:

Increasing Costs

The costs of maintaining automated regulatory compliance are skyrocketing, owing to new regulations proliferating frequently, and new compliance solutions emerging in the market. Rapidly increasing costs create a dilemma in the minds of companies, especially SMBs, whether the costs outweigh the benefits of continuous compliance. You need to compare various solutions available in the market based on features and costs before choosing a solution that is cost-effective.

Changing Cyber Landscape

Being compliant does not mean that you have achieved complete cyber security. Just checking off compliance requirements or implementing strong control, or passing an audit, does not mean that the compliance journey is complete. The cyber landscape is constantly changing and at the end of the day, human oversight is necessary to ensure that new and existing regulations and trends are being addressed.

How to Achieve Continuous Compliance?

What is the approach to maintaining continuous compliance? Going through the compliance journey is well worth the effort. There are some key steps that will lead to successful compliance management.

Identify And Understand Compliance Standards

The first step towards continuous compliance is understanding the policies or standards that you need to comply with. These standards or policies vary dramatically depending on the location, industry, and target customers. For example, healthcare organizations need to adhere to HIPAA guidelines; businesses that serve EU citizens must comply with GDPR; and cloud service providers must comply with SOC 2 policies.

Once you are sure which standard or policy applies to your business, you can start aligning its requirements to your organization. If regulatory or customer requirements require multiple frameworks, then mapping each standard's requirements will help minimize duplicate efforts.

Perform Risk Assessments And Establish Controls

Once the relevant compliance standards have been identified, you can measure how close you are to achieving them. To measure how close you are to achieving, the first step is to audit every asset, system, process, and third-party relationship that could impact compliance.

The next step is to evaluate the compliance gaps in all these entities. The final step is to enact the controls needed to close the gaps and bring the organization into compliance. They could be new processes or even as simple as training programs.

Monitor Continuously

With the right controls in place, you must monitor your compliance continuously. Compliance monitoring is not a one-time process, continuous compliance monitoring is required for every control mechanism that you implement to close compliance gaps.

Activity logs can be used to determine what normal activity means and to highlight unusual activity. Alerts and notifications can tell a process owner what actions to take.

Document Everything

Every decision and incident at every step in the compliance process must be documented. Proper documentation helps process owners to learn from past incidents to improve decision-making and long-term planning. Documentation also helps people learn how their actions impact compliance and how non-compliance affects the business.

This is important because compliance ownership is not concentrated on the IT department. Everyone on the team is assigned specific responsibilities that they need to understand and acknowledge.

Best Practices to Setup Continuous Compliance

Best Practices to Set Up Continuous Compliance
Conduct internal audits or assessments
Retain a security personnel
Set up a org wide training and awareness program
Documentation
Secure all endpoints and IoT devices
Implement strong identity and authentication
Develop a data compliance governance strategy
Implement the right policies

Security Compliance Reporting in DevOps

Security compliance reporting in DevOps involves the generation and presentation of compliance reports to demonstrate adherence to security policies, regulations, and industry standards. Key aspects of this process include:

- **Automated Reporting**: Generate compliance reports automatically at various stages of the DevOps pipeline, including code analysis, infrastructure provisioning, and deployment. Use tools and scripts to collect compliance data and create structured reports.
- **Policy Validation**: Ensure that compliance reports include results of policy validation checks against predefined security policies and standards. Highlight any non-compliance issues, vulnerabilities, or violations.
- **Auditor-Friendly:** Format reports in a way that is easily understandable to auditors and compliance teams. Include clear explanations of compliance status and issues, as well as remediation steps.

- **Continuous Monitoring**: Implement continuous monitoring for security compliance to provide real-time insights into the security posture. This allows for immediate action on compliance violations.
- **Integration with CI/CD:** Embed compliance reporting into the CI/CD pipeline to automatically assess code and infrastructure changes for compliance before deployment. Ensure that non-compliant changes are flagged and reported.
- **Historical Tracking**: Maintain historical compliance reports to track changes and improvements over time. This helps in trend analysis and demonstrating progress in compliance efforts.
- **Customization**: Tailor compliance reports to specific regulatory requirements (e.g., GDPR, PCI DSS) and internal security policies. Customize reports to address unique compliance needs.
- **Documentation**: Keep comprehensive records of compliance reports, including details of security checks, remediation actions, and approvals. Documentation is essential for audits and regulatory compliance.

- **User Access Control:** Implement access controls and permissions to restrict access to compliance reports, ensuring that only authorized personnel can view and modify them.
- **Alerting and Notifications**: Configure automated alerts and notifications for critical compliance issues or changes in compliance status. This ensures timely response and remediation.
- **Alignment with DevOps Processes**: Integrate security compliance reporting seamlessly into the DevOps workflow. Ensure that developers, operations teams, and security personnel are all aligned with compliance requirements.
- **Executive Dashboards:** Create executive-level dashboards that provide a high-level overview of compliance status and key security metrics for senior management and stakeholders.

Security compliance reporting plays a vital role in demonstrating that DevOps practices prioritize security and adhere to regulatory and internal standards. These reports provide transparency and evidence of compliance efforts, which is essential for regulatory audits and maintaining trust with customers and partners.

CHAPTER 14

Future DevOps Trends and Emerging Technologies

Amongst the handful of worthy trends that we have experienced as new age, one of them is undoubtedly the adoption of DevOps industry trends. As we go further in time, it has become quite obvious that DevOps has become a house name amongst the top efficient Agile frameworks. A larger percentage of robust organizations are adopting the DevOps methodology to streamline their operational efficiency and get faster and better results. Modern-day enterprises are quite-aware of the technology services that are currently on trend when it comes to modernizing environments.

With that being said, the new age trends in DevOps have seen a consistent rise in its usage. It is steadily growing in its recognition because of the changes in demands and complexities of modern-day software. Companies today require a diverse set of platforms and operating systems. It is more about taking a business to greater heights and taking advantage of technology rather than doing things in a stipulated way.

The latest technology trends in DevOps work upon the best practices to aid in driving the performance of an enterprise in a modern economy driven by digital advancement. It provides companies with a new way of delivering value to customers at a fast rate. A large number of organizations are realizing the true potential of DevOps regarding overall performance and operational efficiency.

How DevOps Has Transformed in the Past Decade

DevOps as a wholesome framework was first developed by Patrick Dubois. Regarded as the founding father of DevOps, his methodologies and the latest DevOps market trends have been extensively used by organizations worldwide. Let us delve into the history of DevOps to comprehend how it brought about a digital transformation into one of the most renowned work structure designs globally: -

- **2007:** It was in 2007 when the idea of DevOps first came into being. Patrick Dubois had started working on an extensive data center migration where he was responsible for the testing of software. Although he had experienced many hurdles during this project, starting from continuously vacillating from the development side to be operational side, he realized that a large portion of his time and effort was wasted in navigating between project development and project operations. It is in this year that he began considering bridging the gap between these two worlds.

- **2008:** In 2008, an Agile conference was conducted in Toronto, Canada, where Andrew Shafer had attempted to conduct a meeting session named "Agile Infrastructure". Despite having received a large amount of negative feedback, Shafer decided not to show up to even his session. However, Patrick hunted him down at the conference because he was excited to finally meet a person who thought along the same lines as him. They even decided to create a discussion group for numerous people who wanted to share their ideas and thoughts that would bring about a proper solution to the seemingly wide gap between operations and development.

- **2009:** During the initial stage, there were very few people who came forth with ideas regarding this perspective. However, things took a turn on a positive note when Paul Hammond and John Allspaw conducted a conference entitled "10+ Deploys a Day: Dev and Ops Cooperation at Flickr." Patrick, who had watched the streaming video of this presentation, was highly satisfied with it because it resonated with his views. He was so motivated by this meeting that he arranged a congregation of developers and system administrators to discuss ways that will help bridge the gap between development and operations this event was called DevOps days. It is from this term that this agile framework originated because of users on Twitter using the hashtag #DevOps. By this time, enterprises had slowly already begun thinking about implementing this Framework into their work structure to achieve maximum operational efficiency

- **2011:** In March 2011, Cameron Haight of Gartner first presented his predictions for DevOps in the future. It was a positive Outlook that many other members drew inspiration. Companies extensively begin implementing this framework into their work structure regardless of how big or small scale they are.

This is how DevOps has grown since last 2007:

1. **Emergence of DevOps (2007-2010):** DevOps emerged as a response to the challenges of traditional software development and operations silos. Early adopters, like Flickr and Etsy, began pioneering DevOps practices. Concepts like "Infrastructure as Code" and "Continuous Integration/Continuous Deployment (CI/CD)" gained traction.

2. **Rise of Automation (2010-2015):** Automation became a central theme in DevOps. Tools like

Puppet, Chef, Ansible, and Jenkins empowered teams to automate provisioning, configuration management, and deployment. This period also saw the development of containerization technology, with Docker leading the way.

3. **Expansion of DevOps Culture (2015-2020):** DevOps transcended tools and processes to become a cultural movement. Organizations realized that a cultural shift, emphasizing collaboration and shared responsibility, was essential for DevOps success. The term "DevSecOps" emerged, highlighting the integration of security into DevOps workflows.

4. **Cloud-Native and Microservices (2015-2023):** The adoption of cloud-native architectures and microservices gained momentum. Kubernetes became the de facto container orchestration platform. DevOps practices adapted to the cloud-native landscape, with a focus on scalability, resilience, and automation.

5. **Security-First DevOps (2020-2023):** Security

became an integral part of DevOps practices. "DevSecOps" evolved beyond a buzzword to a necessity. Organizations integrated security checks into CI/CD pipelines, implemented secure coding practices, and automated security testing.

6. **AIOps and AI Integration (2020-2023)**: The integration of Artificial Intelligence (AI) and Machine Learning (ML) into DevOps processes revolutionized monitoring, alerting, and anomaly detection. AIOps solutions improved incident response and resource optimization.

7. **GitOps and Infrastructure as Code (IaC) (2020-2023):** GitOps, which uses Git as a single source of truth for infrastructure and application definitions, gained popularity. Infrastructure as Code (IaC) became a standard practice for managing and provisioning infrastructure.

8. **Remote and Distributed Teams (2020-2023):** The COVID-19 pandemic accelerated the adoption of remote work, impacting DevOps

practices. Teams adapted to distributed work environments, relying on collaboration tools and remote-friendly DevOps workflows.

9. **Compliance Automation (2020-2023)**: Compliance automation tools and practices emerged to streamline regulatory compliance in DevOps pipelines. Organizations automated compliance checks, audits, and reporting to meet industry and regulatory standards.

10. **DevOps for Edge and IoT (2023 and Beyond):** As edge computing and IoT (Internet of Things) ecosystems grow, DevOps is expanding to support these environments. DevOps for edge and IoT involves managing distributed, resource-constrained systems efficiently.

DevOps has come a long way from its inception, evolving into a holistic approach that combines culture, automation, collaboration, and security. The past decade has seen its integration with emerging technologies, cultural shifts, and a relentless pursuit of efficiency, agility, and quality in software delivery. Looking ahead, DevOps will continue to evolve in response to new technologies and changing business needs.

Top 7 DevOps Trends to Look Up in Future

1. **DevSecOps**

   With security being one of the most significant concerns in the digital age, enterprises have integrated the DevSecOps lifecycle to enhance it further. It has been used for streamlining governance and observability as well.

   The main idea that DevSecOps stands for is the shift-left approach that security should follow instead of it being an afterthought. As per the latest DevSecOps trends, around 40% of Enterprises conduct the DAST test, 50% conduct the SAST test, and the rest scans dependencies and containers.

One very stark example that we can consider is Pokemon Go. Although Pokemon Go is one of the major game-changing phenomena in the gaming industry, it began to show some liability problems upon its initial launch. With over 800 million downloads by minor users all over the world, they were responsible for the protection of their privacy as per the GDPR rules. However, there was a twist in the tale. Pokemon go partnered with Niantic for its development, with whom it shared responsibilities regarding security compliance and development. Therefore, although a percentage of childcare security compliance, as well as the backend operations, went to Pokemon go, the application as a whole was governed by Niantic.

With the significant amount of shared responsibility and third-party data, instilling collaboration and security culture became a predominant practice. This led to the company adopting DevSecOps integrated automation when it came to security checks instead of manual monitoring of application privacy from the very first stage. This is how the cultural paradigm of Pokemon go helped protect the privacy of billions of children.

2. Serverless Computing

Serverless computing is a way to develop and run services and applications without taking servers into consideration. These applications do not need the managing of servers because they are built that way from the very developmental stage of the app. Over the years, it has come to be a widely used innovative approach to software deployment. As a matter of fact, the serverless market is estimated to reach $30 billion by the year 2030. Additionally, more than 50% of Enterprises that have cloud-based courses have integrated serverless computing in their systems.

The DevOps process has greatly benefited from the serverless computing approach. With added operability, it has successfully bridged the gap between Development and Operations. It also helped generate the DevOps pipeline code without needing the host to develop, test, and deploy.

One stark example is Autodesk, a company that specializes in designing software for Architecture, Engineering, Construction, and Manufacturing. Autodesk has successfully streamlined faster development and facilitated quicker deployment by expanding its AWS footprints. One downside of using AWS is that it still needed a manual process that would take a minimum of two weeks to complete. With the growing number of accounts, it was difficult for Autodesk to sustain its optimum performance and work efficiency. This was when they decided to opt for AWS Dynamodb and AWS Lambda, which became an integral part of their serverless transformation. This significantly helped

Autodesk to shorten the total time required for account creation from two whole weeks to a matter of ten minutes only.

3. Microservices Architecture

Microservice architecture often referred to as microservices, is currently being extensively used in the IT sector. Customized to accommodate the latest DevOps market trends, it has successfully broken down the age-old mammoth-sized applications into more manageable pieces that are smaller. Successfully simplified development testing as well as deployment in operations. It has also streamlined the consistent and frequent delivery of software and applications. It has been easier and simpler to facilitate the DevOps processes and principles to improve the Holistic quality of products.

A popular example would be Coca-Cola which has produced over 3800 products on a global scale. Essentially the company used a legacy-based architecture that connects every entity belonging to various continents. Supporting their ever-increasing growth, however, became a major challenge. This is where the IT teams of Coca-Cola decided to use a DevOps-based approach that involved the use of microservices. This is one of the new trends in DevOps that helps create a separate area for concerns and reusable modules that help enhance the agility as well as the speed of deploying the product. Therefore, with microservice architecture, there was a significant reduction of data flow in the network, leading them to gain more time for scaling up to support more freestyle machines within a matter of minutes from weeks.

4. AIOPS

MLOps and AIOps are two of the most renowned trending DevOps tools. They have been estimated to become a 40.91 billion dollar entity by the year 2026. Essential to optimize the DevOps operations to reap the benefits of high quality and quick release where MLOps and AIOps are important role-players. AIOps help automates IT processes and operations, whereas MLOps strengthens the development system of machine learning. Therefore, with AIOps, it is easy to identify the main cause of the problems that hamper operational productivity, and with MLOps, it is easy to optimize operations and enhance productivity.

This is one of the most widely used DevOps future trends, which has also been integrated into a platform named DRYiCE IntelliOps, developed by HCL. As a solution that addresses the full stack AIOps of the Enterprise as well as its observability requirements, it specializes in transforming the customers of HCL from reactive to proactive. They carried this out with the help of incident management and also by providing more visibility into the infrastructure. Moogsoft has supported this translation of customers into Agile business practitioners without HCL incurring additional costs of operations. This helped in the reduction of help desk tickets by 62%, MTTR by 33%, and also streamlined hassle-free cloud migration

5. Low Code Applications

Many robust enterprises have adopted a low-code DevOps approach which has been quite beneficial for teams. The low-code approach enables agility that provides every organization with a huge competitive edge in the demanding and fast-paced software market. Low-code platforms help companies and enterprises build applications without any export coding knowledge. This helps non-technical professionals to also have a hand in developing software via a visual interface that entirely manages the app development process. It helps users develop their logic and workflow just by dragging and dropping elements. This is one of the renowned DevOps future trends that has helped speed up the process of development and deployment just by creating simplistic and user-friendly applications.

There are many programming tools that are tasked with automating the deployment applications by readily interfacing with low-code platforms. They have also significantly helped with crucial DevOps practices like version control, QA, and even build validation. Being one of the best 2020 DevOps trends, the single-platform approach of this trend that has provided a "no" or a "low" code has also significantly helped DevOps teams work more efficiently, reducing complexity as a whole. The very term 'low code' means having to give lesser emphasis on coding, whereas DevOps means efficient collaboration. Therefore, an amalgamation of the two is bound to enhance development and deployment.

6. GitOps

GitOps happens to be one of the best DevOps new trends that have been added to the DevOps workflow. It helps control, monitor, and automate infrastructure. Based on the Kubernetes paradigm, it has given IT operation managers and developers the ability to utilize Git for collecting and deploying several applications. GitOps takes all of the best DevOps practices, such as collaboration, version control Al, compliance, and CI/CD, into consideration and applies them to the infrastructure of automation. It additionally emphasizes increasing releases as well as consistent delivery to create, test, and deploy software fastly and with maximum efficiency.

One great example is the finance form called Mettle, powered by NatWest. It seeks to offer customers of small businesses applications that streamline payments by speeding them up and effectively managing their finances. Therefore, ensuring that every service is consistently running 24/7 is imperative in their business infrastructure. In one instance, the engineering team of Mettle was challenged to find a solution where they could deploy the newest features at the fastest pace without compromising on the CI/CD pipeline security as well as reliability. To enable this, Mettle had to partner with Weaveworks to adopt the GITOps approach. It helped Mettle to develop a self-service program that enabled engineers to focus more on delivering value via innovation without any help from the platform team assistance. This helped increase production by 50% and deployment by 25%.

7. **Kubernetes**

Kubernetes, often abbreviated as K8, is an extensible and portable open-source platform that helps in managing containerized services and workloads. It provides a continuous and autonomous container-based ecosystem for integration, allowing developers to scale up or down on the resources. This is one of the prime reasons why it has become one of the top DevOps trends in 2023. Newly, 48% of developers have turned to Kubernetes for container integration. On top of all, Kubernetes helps facilitate cross-functional action and make sure that there is minimum deployment downtime to align with the standard and the best DevOps practices.

A great example of this is Nordstrom Inc., an American luxury departmental store that is headquartered in Seattle. As in the e-commerce industry, agility, speed, and a phenomenal customer experience were vital to that company's principles. Therefore they began using Kubernetes to incorporate a complete DevOps transformation, the deployment of pipelines, as well as the implementation of consistent integration. This helped them considerably reduce the time required for deployment from 3 months to a matter of 30 minutes, in addition to enhancing operational efficiency.

DevOps and Artificial Intelligence

AI in DevOps involves the use of machine learning

(ML) and other artificial intelligence technologies to automate and optimize the software development and delivery process. This includes everything from automating testing and deployment processes to improving resource management and enhancing security.

By leveraging the use of AI in DevOps, organizations benefit from the improved speed, accuracy, and reliability of the software development lifecycle. Which, in turn, leads to faster deployments, reduced errors, and increased overall productivity.

What is artificial intelligence?

Artificial Intelligence (AI) refers to the development of computer systems that perform tasks in a manner that simulates human intelligence. These computer systems, or machines, are programmed to perform tasks such as learning, reasoning, and problem-solving. AI is quickly becoming incorporated within many processes across a range of industries due to its ability to automate tasks, reduce errors, and make fast, intelligent decisions based on data analysis.

Types of AI used in DevOps

There are several types of AI used in DevOps, including:

- Machine learning
- Natural language processing
- Computer vision
- Chatbots and virtual assistants

The fusion of DevOps and Artificial Intelligence (AI) represents a pivotal moment in the evolution of software development and operations. Here are key points, use cases, examples, and future prospects for DevOps and AI:

1. **Automation Augmented by AI**:
    - AI technologies, such as Machine Learning

(ML) and Natural Language Processing (NLP), enhance automation capabilities in DevOps.

- AI-driven automation can predict and respond to issues, optimize workflows, and reduce manual interventions.

2. **Predictive Analytics in DevOps:**
   - AI analyzes vast datasets from DevOps tools to predict potential bottlenecks, failures, or security threats.
   - Example: Predicting infrastructure resource demands and automatically scaling resources based on AI-driven forecasts.

3. **AI-Powered Testing and QA:**
   - AI-driven testing tools can generate test cases, analyze test results, and improve test coverage.
   - Example: Test case generation based on code changes and historical test data.

4. **Anomaly Detection and Security:**
   - AI monitors for abnormal behavior and security threats in real time.
   - Example: Detecting unusual access patterns in cloud environments and flagging them as potential security incidents.

5. **Chatbots and Virtual Assistants:**
   - AI-driven chatbots assist DevOps teams by answering questions, providing documentation, and executing routine tasks.
   - Example: A chatbot that deploys and monitors applications based on natural language commands.

6. **Infrastructure Optimization:**
   - AI optimizes resource allocation in cloud environments, reducing costs and improving performance.
   - Example: AI-driven recommendations for resource scaling and utilization.

7. **Natural Language Processing (NLP):**
   - NLP-powered tools extract insights from unstructured data like logs and documentation.
   - Example: Analyzing logs and identifying patterns or anomalies using NLP.

8. **Continuous Feedback Loop**:
   - AI analyzes user feedback and telemetry data to provide insights into software performance.
   - Example: AI-driven sentiment analysis of user reviews to prioritize feature improvements.

9. **Executive Dashboards:**
   - AI-generated insights feed into executive-level dashboards, providing a high-level overview of DevOps performance and security metrics

How to implement AI in DevOps

Using AI for CI/CD

One of the most common ways to use AI in DevOps is for continuous integration and continuous delivery or deployment (CI/CD). AI helps to automate the process of building, testing, and deploying code, so that any changes that pass appropriate tests can then be integrated into the existing codebase and deployed to production environments right away. This process can help reduce the risk of errors and improves the overall quality of the software being developed.

Automating testing with AI

AI can also be used to automate testing processes, which is critical for organizations that want to achieve continuous delivery. By using AI to automatically run tests on new code, developers can quickly identify and fix any issues that arise, ensuring that the code is ready for deployment as soon as possible. Popular tools for this purpose include Selenium and Water.

Code suggestions

AI can suggest code while developers are typing. These AI-assisted code suggestions can help your team write code more efficiently and release software faster.

Enhancing monitoring and alerting with AI

Another important aspect of DevOps is monitoring and alerting. AI can be used to monitor systems and applications in real-time, detecting potential issues before they become problems. Additionally, AI can be used to automatically generate alerts when specific conditions are met, helping operations teams respond more quickly to incidents and preventing downtime.

Finding the right code reviewers

AI and ML models can be used to help developers

find the right people to review their code and merge requests. These automatic suggested reviewers can help developers receive faster and higher-quality reviews, and reduce context switching.

Incorporating AI for continuous improvement

AI can also be used to support continuous improvement efforts within DevOps organizations. By analyzing data from various sources, such as logs, performance metrics, and user feedback, AI can identify trends and patterns that may indicate areas where improvements can be made. This information can then be used to guide future development efforts and optimize the software delivery process.

Using AI for anomaly detection

AI can be used to detect anomalies in log data or other sources of data. This can help DevOps teams identify potential issues before they become critical, reducing downtime and improving product quality.

Root cause analysis with AI

AI can be used to perform root cause analysis on issues that occur in the development process. This can help DevOps teams identify the underlying cause of the problem and take steps to prevent it from happening again.

Understanding vulnerabilities with AI

AI can be used to summarize vulnerabilities and suggest a way to mitigate them. This can help developers and security analysts remediate vulnerabilities faster and more efficiently, and uplevel their skills so they can write more secure code in the future.

Future Prospects (Beyond 2023):

- AI will play an increasingly central role in DevOps, driving autonomous operations and decision-making.
- More AI-driven DevOps tools will emerge, offering solutions for problem-solving, optimization, and real-time incident response.

- The integration of AI and DevOps will extend into edge computing environments and support IoT ecosystems.
- Ethical AI practices will become critical in DevOps, ensuring responsible and transparent use of AI technologies.

Use Case: AI-Enhanced Incident Response:

- AI analyzes logs and monitoring data to detect anomalies indicative of security incidents.
- When an incident is detected, AI can autonomously take actions, such as isolating affected systems or rolling back changes.
- Human intervention is only required for complex or ambiguous cases.

The future of DevOps and AI promises to be transformative, with AI-driven automation becoming an integral part of DevOps workflows. This convergence will lead to more efficient, secure, and responsive software development and operations practices.

BlockChain and DevOps Integration

The era of dynamic user-generated content employed extensively in e-commerce was ushered in by Web2. Web3, on the other hand, which is supported by blockchain technology, ushers in a new era of decentralization by allowing users to own their data. Web3 businesses like ConsenSys provide new equipment that promises various security and productivity advantages when used with standard DevOps approaches.

Web3 can bring the benefits of blockchain and

DevOps working together, albeit in its early stages. This article examines how DevOps approaches, practices, tools, and blockchain technology collaborate to develop Web3 solutions.

DevOps is a broad term that describes a culture, philosophy, development approach, processes, and software development technology. DevOps emphasizes collaboration, automation, predictable outcomes, shorter delivery cycles, and quicker client feedback to improve the quality of software delivery. A distributed, unchangeable ledger technology is called blockchain. In a blockchain ledger, transactions and other events are recorded in decentralized "blocks" that are part of the ledger's network. After then, a transaction recorded on a blockchain cannot be changed.

Since network nodes rather than centralized servers power most blockchain networks, they are decentralized. Additionally, because decentralized blockchains are permissionless, anyone can access them and participate in their networks.

How Do DevOps and Blockchain Complement Each Other?

Through the DevOps cycle, the software delivery chain is continuously improved. Its best practices can make it easier to create blockchain technology at different phases and with different tools. Utilizing current DevOps tools and methodologies, containerization, automation, and short development iterations will improve blockchain development.

On the other hand, blockchain technology enables improved service and data delivery due to immutability, security, smart contracts, and other capabilities. It can also raise the bar for DevOps delivery by ensuring quality and eliminating ambiguity.

The Future of Web3 and DevOps

A new generation of blockchain-based DevOps tools, processes, and practices may be created through Web3. Decentralized, distributed, secure code repositories for global commerce and open-source cooperation are a couple of examples. Examples of such code repositories are Radicle and Ellcrys.

Web3 will also require specialized programming languages with a broad library offering and the ability to work around blockchain constraints. One example of such a programming language is Solidity. Programmers may construct, test, and run their apps on the Ethereum Virtual Machines using the development framework truffle (EVM).

Although sender verification is not always possible with Web2 apps, message content verification is. Trusted nodes that can verify the sender offer blockchain technology an additional layer of protection.

Web3 will increase developer trust and security while enabling anybody to examine the quality and intent of a piece of software thanks to the immutable ledger and smart contracts. Tools like Diligence can be used to audit these smart contracts. Quorum Key

Manager is one of the extra tools that can help with secret and key management.

Future Possibilities (Beyond 2023):

- The integration of Blockchain and DevOps will continue to evolve, potentially leading to entirely decentralized and trustless DevOps ecosystems.
- Blockchain-based DevOps solutions may become more mainstream, particularly in industries with stringent security and compliance requirements.

Example: Blockchain-Based Release Management:

- A DevOps team uses a Blockchain network to record and manage software releases.
- Each release is cryptographically signed and recorded on the blockchain, providing an immutable record of when and how the release occurred.
- Any changes made to the release, such as rollbacks or patches, are also recorded on the

blockchain, creating a transparent history of release management.

The integration of Blockchain and DevOps is still in its early stages, but it holds the potential to significantly improve the security, transparency, and trustworthiness of software development and operations processes. As Blockchain technology matures and gains wider adoption, its impact on DevOps practices is likely to grow.

The Role of DevOps in Edge Computing

Edge computing is a distributed architecture that moves applications as close as possible to where actions are performed—and, essentially, where the data is created.

This is a transformational approach to how enterprises can run applications and services. Internet of Things-connected devices and assets—such as driverless vehicles, mining equipment, commercial vessels, oil rigs, smart parking meters, fitness trackers, and household appliances—are dependent on edge applications, but it is the widespread rollout of 5G that will accelerate businesses from all industries and allow them to introduce new disruptive applications and services.

The integration of DevOps with Edge Computing represents a potent synergy that effectively addresses the distinctive challenges associated with deploying and managing applications at the network's edge. This fusion allows organizations to harness the unique advantages of both technologies, resulting in more efficient, responsive, and dependable systems.

1. **Streamlined Development and Deployment:** The integration of DevOps practices with Edge Computing streamlines the development and deployment of edge applications. DevOps methodologies, with their emphasis on automation, continuous integration, and

continuous deployment, establish a seamless pipeline for creating, testing, and deploying edge applications. This ensures that code changes can be rapidly and consistently pushed out to the edge, promoting Swiffer innovation and heightened responsiveness.

2. **Automation for Edge Environments**: Automation serves as a fundamental pillar of both DevOps and Edge Computing. By incorporating DevOps automation tools and practices into edge environments, organizations can eliminate manual, error-prone tasks. This encompasses activities such as provisioning and configuring edge devices, managing containers or virtual machines, and orchestrating application deployments. Automation guarantees uniformity, diminishes human error, and accelerates the delivery of applications to the edge.

3. **Continuous Monitoring and Feedback:** DevOps underscores the importance of continuous monitoring for applications and infrastructure, enabling teams to detect and

address issues in real-time. When applied to Edge Computing, this practice becomes indispensable for maintaining the health and performance of edge deployments. DevOps tools for monitoring and observability can be extended to edge environments, offering invaluable insights into the status and behavior of applications at the edge.

4. **Security and Compliance:** Security holds critical significance in both DevOps and Edge Computing. Integrating these technologies enables organizations to consistently apply best security practices across cloud and edge environments. This encompasses practices such as scanning code for vulnerabilities, implementing access controls, and managing encryption protocols. Furthermore, compliance policies can be uniformly enforced, ensuring that edge deployments align with regulatory requirements.

5. **Scalability and Flexibility**: DevOps practices like containerization and microservices

architectures are ideally suited for edge deployments. These technologies facilitate the breakdown of applications into smaller, more manageable components, enabling easier scaling and adaptability to evolving demands at the edge. Consequently, applications can evolve dynamically to meet the requirements of dynamic edge environments.

In conclusion, the integration of DevOps with Edge Computing empowers organizations to efficiently develop, deploy, and manage applications at the edge. By amalgamating the principles of automation, continuous improvement, and security, businesses can unlock the full potential of edge technologies. This enables the delivery of faster, more reliable services to end-users, while successfully adapting to the challenges presented by the ever-evolving digital landscape.

The Impact of DevOps on IoT

Security

DevOps has a significant impact on IoT (Internet of Things) security by fostering a proactive and holistic approach to securing IoT devices and ecosystems. By integrating security practices into the DevOps workflow, organizations can address IoT security challenges more effectively. DevOps enables continuous security testing, vulnerability assessment, and automated patch management for IoT devices. It also facilitates the rapid deployment of security updates, reducing exposure to vulnerabilities. Furthermore, DevOps practices promote collaboration between security teams and development teams, ensuring that security is considered throughout the entire IoT product lifecycle. In a rapidly evolving IoT landscape, DevOps plays a pivotal role in safeguarding IoT devices, data, and networks from emerging threats and vulnerabilities.

Implementation of DevOps for IoT Security:

Implementing DevOps for IoT security involves several key practices and considerations. Firstly, it requires integrating security testing and validation into the CI/CD pipeline to identify vulnerabilities early in the development process. Automated security testing tools can scan IoT device firmware and software for common vulnerabilities, ensuring that security is a non-negotiable part of the release process.

Additionally, security should be treated as code, meaning that security policies, configurations, and access controls are managed through version-controlled scripts and templates. Infrastructure as code (IaC) principles can be applied to IoT device provisioning and configuration, ensuring consistency and security across a fleet of devices.

Furthermore, DevOps enables continuous monitoring and threat detection for IoT devices. With real-time telemetry and anomaly detection, security teams can quickly identify suspicious activities and respond to potential threats, reducing the risk of data breaches or device compromise.

Example: Securing Industrial IoT (IIoT) Devices:

Consider an IIoT scenario where manufacturing machines are equipped with IoT sensors to monitor performance and gather data for predictive maintenance. DevOps practices can be applied to secure these devices:

- Security Testing: DevOps integrates automated security testing into the CI/CD pipeline for IIoT device software. Vulnerabilities are identified and patched before deployment.
- Infrastructure as Code: IIoT device configurations and access control policies are managed as code. Any changes are tracked, reviewed, and deployed consistently across all devices.
- Continuous Monitoring: DevOps enables continuous monitoring of IIoT devices. Anomalies, such as unexpected data patterns or unauthorized access attempts, trigger alerts for

immediate investigation.

- Rapid Response: When a security incident is detected, DevOps allows for rapid incident response. Security patches or configuration changes can be pushed to affected devices swiftly, reducing the impact of security breaches.

By implementing DevOps practices, IoT environments can maintain a high level of security, ensuring the integrity of data and the uninterrupted operation of critical industrial processes.

Database DevOps

Many companies use automated processes (like pipelines) to manage their software code, deploy it, test it, and set up their computer systems. However, when it comes to working with databases (which store important data), they often don't use these same automated methods. Instead, they handle databases in a separate way, and this causes a lot of problems. It's now time to start using automation for databases too.

What is Database DevOps?

Database DevOps is a method that helps speed up and improve the way software is created and released. It focuses on making it easier for developers and operations teams to work together.

When you want to create reliable products, it's essential to make sure that databases and software work well together. With DevOps, you can build and launch both the software and the database using the same setup.

We use DevOps techniques to handle database tasks. We make changes based on feedback from the stages where we deliver and develop applications. This helps ensure a smooth delivery process.

Database DevOps Features :

Database DevOps products typically have the following features:

- Version control
- Source control
- Automated deployment
- Release management
- Script validation
- Schema maintenance
- Visibility into database changes
- Rollbacks

The Database Bottleneck (Source: Liquibase)

A 2019 State of Database Deployments in Application Delivery report found that for the second year in a row, database deployments are a bottleneck. 92% of respondents reported difficulty in accelerating database deployments.

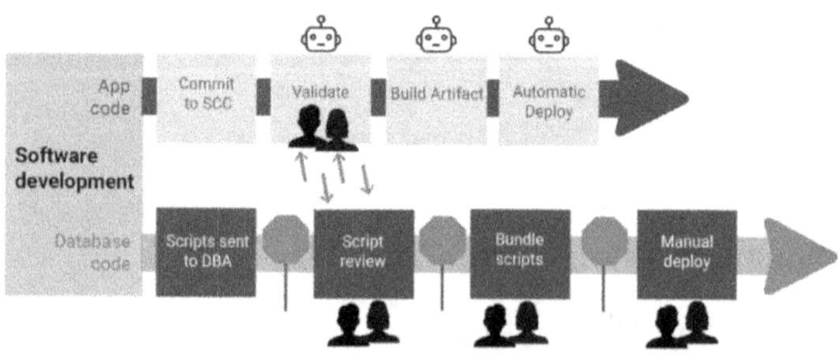

Since database changes follow a manual process, requests for database code reviews are often the last thing holding up a release. Developers understandably get frustrated because the code they wrote a few weeks ago is still in review. The whole database change process is just a blocker.

Now, teams no longer have to wait for DBAs to review the changes until the final phase. It's not only possible but necessary to do this earlier in the process and package all code together.

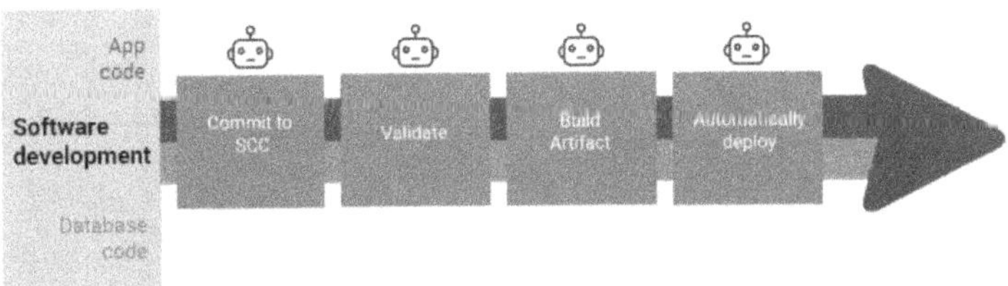

Top Database DevOps Challenges

Database DevOps, while incredibly beneficial, comes with its fair share of challenges. Some of the top challenges in implementing Database DevOps include:

1. Data Synchronization: Keeping development and production databases in sync can be complex.

Changes made to database schemas, data, or configurations need to be accurately synchronized between environments.

2. Data Security: Ensuring that sensitive data is properly protected throughout the DevOps process, especially in non-production environments, is crucial. Masking, encryption, and access control are key considerations.

3. Testing and Validation: Comprehensive testing of database changes is essential. It can be challenging to automate testing procedures for databases, including data validation and performance testing.

4. Schema Evolution: Managing database schema changes and handling backward compatibility while maintaining existing data can be tricky. Ensuring that database changes do not break existing applications is crucial.

5. Version Control: Applying version control to databases and ensuring that database changes are tracked, reviewed, and documented properly can be challenging. Database code should be treated with the same rigor as application code.

6. Manual Processes: Over-reliance on manual processes for database deployments can slow down the DevOps pipeline and introduce errors.

7. Legacy Systems: Integrating Database DevOps practices into legacy systems can be challenging, especially if these systems were not initially designed with DevOps in mind.

8. Cultural and Organizational Changes: Implementing Database DevOps often requires cultural and organizational shifts, including breaking down silos between development and operations teams, which can be met with resistance.

9. Tooling: Finding and implementing the right

tools for Database DevOps can be daunting, as the ecosystem is vast and rapidly evolving.

10. Compliance and Auditing: Meeting regulatory requirements and ensuring that database changes are audited and compliant with industry standards is an ongoing challenge.

11. Performance Tuning: Optimizing database performance in a DevOps environment requires continuous monitoring and fine-tuning, which can be resource-intensive.

12. Rollback and Recovery: Having effective rollback and recovery procedures in place is crucial in case a database change causes unexpected issues in production.

Successfully addressing these challenges involves a combination of technology, processes, and a cultural shift toward collaboration and automation between development and operations teams.

How can DevOps help in solving the above

challenges?

DevOps practices can help address many of the challenges associated with Database DevOps by promoting collaboration, automation, and a systematic approach to managing database changes. Here's how DevOps can assist in solving the problems mentioned:

1. **Data Synchronization:** Automation Tool: Ansible Use Ansible playbooks to automate database schema updates and ensure consistent configurations across environments. Example: Use Ansible to deploy database schema changes, ensuring that development and production databases remain synchronized.

2. **Data Security:** Automation Tool: Hashi Corp Vault Hashi Corp Vault automates secrets management and encryption, enhancing data security. Example: Store and retrieve database credentials securely from HashiCorp Vault, ensuring sensitive data remains protected.

3. **Testing and Validation:** Automation Tool: Jenkins Integrate Jenkins as part of the CI/CD pipeline to automate database testing. Example: Implement automated database testing scripts within Jenkins jobs to validate data integrity and performance.

4. **Schema Evolution:** Version Control Tool: GitUse Git for version control of database schema scripts, enabling efficient collaboration. Example: Maintain a Git repository for tracking and managing database schema changes, allowing for easy rollback if needed.

5. **Version Control:** Database Version Control Tool: Liquibase Liquibase is designed for database schema versioning and change management. Example: Use Liquibase to track and deploy database schema changes with version control, enabling a structured approach to database evolution.

6. **Manual Processes:** Automation Tool: Chef Chef automates infrastructure provisioning, including database setups. Example: Use Chef recipes to automate database server configurations, reducing manual intervention.

7. **Legacy Systems:** Gradual Transition Tool: Docker Containerization with Docker can facilitate gradual migration to modern Database DevOps practices. Example: Containerize legacy databases using Docker to make them more manageable and integrate them into the DevOps pipeline.

8. **Cultural and Organizational Changes:** Collaboration Tool: Slack Use communication tools like Slack to foster collaboration among development and operations teams. Example: Create dedicated Slack channels for cross-functional teams to encourage communication and knowledge sharing.

9. **Tooling: Database Deployment Tool:** AWS RDSAWS Relational Database Service (RDS) simplifies database management and can be integrated into DevOps workflows. Example: Use AWS RDS to provision, scale, and manage databases in a DevOps-friendly manner.

10. **Compliance and Auditing: Compliance Tool:** Sysdig Secure Sysdig Secure provides automated compliance checks and auditing for containerized environments. Example: Implement Sysdig Secure to continuously monitor and audit containerized databases for compliance with industry standards.

11. **Performance Tuning:** Monitoring Tool: Prometheus Prometheus offers robust monitoring capabilities for database performance. Example: Set up Prometheus for real-time monitoring of database metrics and establish alerting to address performance issues promptly.

12. **Rollback and Recovery:** Backup and Restore Tool: AWS Backup AWS Backup automates data backup and recovery for AWS resources, including databases. Example: Configure automated backups with AWS Backup to ensure quick recovery in case of unexpected issues caused by database changes.

By combining DevOps practices with these tools and examples, organizations can enhance their Database DevOps capabilities, streamline database management, and achieve more efficient, secure, and reliable database operations.

Top Database DevOps Tools

Open-Source Database DevOps Tools:

1. Liquibase: An open-source tool for database schema version control and change management.
2. Flyway: Another open-source database migration tool that emphasizes simplicity and ease of use.
3. DBDeploy: A database change management tool

that works with plain SQL scripts.

4. SQLAlchemy: A Python SQL toolkit and Object-Relational Mapping (ORM) library that supports database automation and migrations.
5. Docker: While not exclusively a database tool, Docker is often used to containerize databases for easier management and deployment.

6. Gogs/Gitea: Self-hosted Git repository management tools that can be used for version controlling database schema scripts.

Paid Database DevOps Tools:

1. Redgate SQL Toolbelt: A suite of tools for database automation, source control, and database CI/CD.
2. dbForge Studio: A database development and management tool with features for schema change management and version control.
3. Datical: Provides database release automation, version control, and compliance solutions for databases.

4. Octopus Deploy: While primarily a deployment automation tool, it supports database deployments and integrates with many database systems.
5. Toad for Oracle: A database development and management tool that includes features for schema management and automation.
6. AWS Database Migration Service: AWS provides a managed service for migrating and replicating databases, including tools for schema conversion.

7. Microsoft SQL Server Data Tools (SSDT): A set of tools for database development, schema management, and deployment for SQL Server.
8. IBM UrbanCode Deploy: An application deployment automation tool that supports database deployment automation and integrations with various databases.
9. Quest SharePlex: A data replication and change data capture (CDC) tool that helps with database synchronization and high availability.

These tools cater to different database systems, such

as MySQL, PostgreSQL, Oracle, SQL Server, and more. The choice of tool depends on your specific database technology, project requirements, and budget. It's essential to evaluate each tool's features, compatibility, and community/support when selecting the right one for your Database DevOps needs.

Real-World Examples

1. **Netflix:**
    - Netflix is a pioneer in using DevSecOps practices to secure its streaming platform.
    - They employ automated security testing, continuous monitoring, and real-time anomaly detection to protect customer data and streaming services.
    - Netflix's security team collaborates closely

with development and operations teams to ensure that security is integrated throughout the development lifecycle.

2. **Etsy:**
    - Etsy, an e-commerce platform, has embraced DevSecOps to secure its online marketplace.
    - They use automated security scans to detect vulnerabilities in code and dependencies.
    - Etsy's security team participates in daily stand-ups with development teams, fostering a culture of security awareness and collaboration.
3. **The U.S. Department of Defense (DoD):**
    - The DoD has adopted DevSecOps to enhance the security of its software development and deployment processes.
    - They've implemented DevSecOps practices across various defense projects, emphasizing automated security testing, containerization, and infrastructure as code (IaC) for consistent and secure deployments.

4. **Intuit:**

   - Intuit, the company behind financial software like QuickBooks and TurboTax, uses DevSecOps to protect sensitive financial data.
   - They integrate security checks into their CI/CD pipelines, conduct regular threat modeling, and emphasize secure coding practices.
   - Intuit's approach ensures the security of financial transactions and user data.

5. **Microsoft Azure:**

   - Microsoft's cloud platform, Azure, employs DevSecOps practices to secure its infrastructure and services.
   - They leverage AI and machine learning for real-time threat detection and automated incident response.
   - Azure's DevSecOps initiatives help safeguard customer data and maintain the availability

and reliability of cloud services.

Top 10 Project for Practice

1. **Simple CI/CD Pipeline for a Personal Website:**
    - Implement a CI/CD pipeline with Jenkins or GitLab CI.
    - Add automated testing and code quality checks (e.g., unit tests, linting).

- Incorporate security scans using tools like SonarQube or OWASP Dependency-Check.
- Use IaC (Infrastructure as Code) to define the web server setup for consistency.

2. **Dockerized Web Application:**
   - Containerize a web application using Docker and Docker Compose.
   - Create a Dockerfile for each component (web server, database, etc.).
   - Implement CI/CD for Docker image builds and deployments.
   - Integrate Docker security scanning with tools like Clair or Trivy.

3. **Infrastructure as Code (IaC) for AWS:**
   - Use Terraform or AWS CloudFormation to define cloud resources (e.g., EC2 instances, VPC, RDS).
   - Implement IAM (Identity and Access Management) policies for secure access.
   - Enable encryption for data at rest and in transit.

- Set up AWS Config for compliance monitoring.

4. **Microservices Architecture:**
   - Design a microservices-based application with separate components.
   - Create CI/CD pipelines for each microservice.
   - Implement API security using OAuth 2.0 or JWT.
   - Explore Istio or Linkerd for service mesh security.

5. **Security Automation with Ansible:**
   - Develop Ansible playbooks for automated security tasks (e.g., patch management, user access).

   - Implement configuration management to enforce security policies.
   - Set up Ansible Vault for securing sensitive data.

6. **Kubernetes Cluster Setup:**
   - Deploy a Kubernetes cluster (e.g., Minikube,

AWS EKS, or GKE).

- Use Helm charts to manage application deployments.
- Implement RBAC (Role-Based Access Control) for cluster security.
- Explore network policies to control pod communication.

7. **Continuous Monitoring and Logging:**
   - Deploy Prometheus for monitoring and Grafana for visualization.
   - Configure alerts for key metrics (e.g., high CPU usage, failed logins).
   - Set up ELK stack (Elasticsearch, Logstash, Kibana) for centralized logging.
   - Define log retention policies for compliance.

8. **Web Application Firewall (WAF) Implementation:**
   - Deploy a WAF (e.g., AWS WAF, ModSecurity) in front of a web application.
   - Create WAF rules to mitigate common web-based attacks (e.g., SQL injection, XSS).

- Configure rate limiting and IP blocking policies.
- Monitor WAF logs for suspicious activity.

9. **DevSecOps for Mobile Apps:**
   - Use mobile app scanning tools like MobSF or OWASP ZAP for static analysis.
   - Implement code signing and obfuscation techniques for app security.
   - Set up automated testing for mobile app vulnerabilities.
   - Secure APIs and data storage for mobile apps.

10. **Compliance Automation:**
    - Choose a compliance framework (e.g., CIS, NIST, GDPR).
    - Develop scripts or workflows to automate

compliance checks.

- Integrate compliance checks into the CI/CD pipeline.
- Generate compliance reports and remediate issues automatically.

References

- https://www.izertis.com/en/-/blog/devops-evolution-to-devsecops-and-key-tools
- https://hackernoon.com/the-evolution-of-devops-

to-devsecops-integrating-security-into-the-software-development-lifecycle

- https://blog.softtek.com/en/devsecops-a-new-work-philosophy
- https://www.f5.com/resources/solution-guides/ci-cd-pipeline-security-automation-solution-overview
- https://www.linkedin.com/advice/1/how-can-you-integrate-security-your-devops-workflow
- https://loft.sh/blog/what-does-it-mean-to-scale-a-deployment/#:~:text=Kubernetes%20will%20create%20more%20pods,per%20our%20scale%20action%20above.&text=Kubernetes%20will%20delete%20two%20pods,therefore%2C%20scale%20down%20our%20deployment.
- https://bluexp.netapp.com/blog/cvo-blg-kubernetes-scaling-the-comprehensive-guide-to-scaling-apps
- https://www.chat.openai.com/
- https://www.computer.org/publications/tech-news/trends/effective-secrets-management-best-practices
- https://budibase.com/blog/app-building/how-to-implement-rbac/

- https://www.harness.io/blog/secrets-management-ci-cd
- https://geekflare.com/container-security-scanners/
- https://www.checkpoint.com/cyber-hub/container-security-scanning/#:~:text=A%20container%20scanner%20has%20the,contain%20known%20vulnerabilities%20or%20malware.
- https://www.cflowapps.com/continuous-compliance/
- https://sprinto.com/blog/continuous-compliance/
- https://www.knowledgehut.com/blog/devops/devops-trends
- https://about.gitlab.com/topics/devops/the-role-of-ai-in-devops/
- https://www.devopsschool.com/blog/integrating-blockchain-and-devops/
- https://www.linkedin.com/pulse/edge-computing-devops-5-killer-ways-benefit-from-integration/

www.ingramcontent.com/pod-product-compliance
Lightning Source LLC
Chambersburg PA
CBHW062132160726
48282CB00027B/802
* 9 7 8 9 3 5 9 8 0 7 5 4 6 *